D1134861

Behind the Mountains

OLIVER LA FARGE

HOUGHTON MIFFLIN COMPANY BOSTON

1956 · The Riverside Press Cambridge

Foreword

A BOOK of this kind involves the writer in the dangerous, sometimes deadly, business of "arrangement." The great events of this world are likely to shape themselves in the natural form of plot, drama, and climax; the small incidents of quiet lives tend to the reverse. It is, I think, no betrayal of truth to juxtapose incidents in sequences a trifle apter than occur in real life, since no matter how true the tale, it is worthless if it be not readable.

I have done that, and in a very few instances, not more than three or four, I have also imported into this account items not in fact from the Bacas' experience, but from that of others of similar background. My purpose in this has been greater completeness or the better illustration of a point.

All but three of the chapters in this book appeared originally in *The New Yorker,* with minor differences of treatment. I am deeply indebted to the editors of that magazine, and especially to Messrs. Lobrano and Maxwell, and the late, magnificent Harold Ross. Seldom in my writing life have editors so infuriated me, and never have I known any who could so help a writer accomplish his purpose. This book presented a technical problem; if I have solved it, a good bit of the credit goes to them.

Above I mentioned completeness. One of the aims of this book is to record a fair picture of a way of life that has ceased to exist. Left-wingers will immediately object that relations between the *patrones* and the workers cannot have been as idyllic as they appear here, to which part of my answer is that one must stick to his data, which in this case is the memory of the *patrones*, gilded by time. Another part is that I have been back to Rociada with the Bacas, and seen the shared tears, the embraces, heard the spate of reminiscences, witnessed the unmistakable signs of mutual love.

My debt to the Bacas themselves is, obviously, approximately equal to what value this book may have. It would be stretching the facts only a little to list Consuelo as co-author. All of them pitched in to help. Emilie and Joséphine took time off from the demands of the posts they occupied in Japan to send in reminiscences, Marguerite Carmen made many contributions, and José Albino, called Pino, was a gold mine. I specially thank him for giving me permission to run the second chapter. As to Doña Marguerite, not only was she the source of much material and even of wording, but her realism and the unusual accuracy of her memory again and again enabled me to complete and to visualize fully what I had from the others. When she read these chapters in draft form, her only suggestions for changes were for greater accuracy or to add some lively detail that I had missed.

These remarks make it sound as if we went about this business formally. We did not. The heart of the material, the color and life of it, came in the most delightful way — simply sitting and listening to my wife and my in-laws remembering together. Perhaps the most significant thing I can say about all the Bacas is that never once was any suggestion made that I characterize any of them other than as I saw them, or that I put any item more favorably.

Santa Fe, New Mexico
1955

Contents

Behind the Mountains

I

Wedding at Rociada

VISITORS TO New Mexico do not go to Rociada, where my wife, Consuelo, grew up. Broadly speaking, the name Rociada covers two villages, the embracing ranch, and the valley in which they lie. The valley is high, long, and irregular, walled by the higher mountains of the Sangre de Cristo range, east of Santa Fe and the Pecos, north of Las Vegas, away from everywhere, innocent of paved roads.

Down the middle of the valley runs a clear, fast, noisy stream in which one may take trout. In the lowland along the stream and its tributaries are the farmlands; beyond them are the pastures reaching to the high-wooded knees of the mountains. Behind the crests of the first rugged walls, shaggy with spruce and fir and pine, are the main peaks, with the brown, domed, pure rock of El Ermitaño, snow-powdered until midsummer, as a monument and guardian notching the western sky. The pasture lands carry grass to tickle the belly of a calf or a colt, or to hide a young lamb. They are mountain meadows, embroidered, according to the season, with iris, columbine, Indian paintbrush, tiger lilies, or cardinal flowers.

When a man who lives and works in the arid country that is most of New Mexico, or even in the semi-green irrigated lands along the sand-edged rivers, comes traveling through such a place as Rociada, he feels his being relax and spread out. He experiences something of what happened to the lotus-eaters, wanting to stay always a little longer, let his horses feast, smell the water, and feel the live grass. He moves on because he must, and the next night camps in lower country, where the gravelly soil shows between the single blades of grass, and dry stalks of weeds rattle in the night when the wind stirs.

In the valley of Rociada, the main river runs south from the high peaks, then turns easterly. Where it turns is the village of Rociada; a couple of miles above that is Upper Rociada. These are *placitas,* little plazas. Each consists of a score, more or less, of adobe houses, a church, a store, and a dance hall, grouped inexactly around a central square. Adobe is decorated with whitewash or calcimine only where a porch protects its surface from the harsh winter snows; the rest is left plain. The settlements match the surrounding earth, from which they are built.

Rociada means, roughly, "bedewed." The main and upper settlements were made in a forgotten period by men who were not afraid of the Apache hunting bands that came drifting through that country. Gascón is newer. It was founded by Consuelo's grandfather Jean Pendaries, who came from Gascony. He built his home ranch at the south end of his domain, downstream from the village of

Rociada. José Albino Baca, who married M. Pendaries' daughter Marguerite, and to whom the Pendaries ranch eventually passed, built his house — a big, two-story adobe building with a pitched roof and porches front and back — a mile above the older place and two and a half miles from the village. On a still day when the mill on the Pendaries place, "the lower ranch," was running, one could hear the dull clack of the wooden water wheel from the ranchhouse. Villages and ranches alike are strung along the stream, which has a name — Río Manuelitas — but which Consuelo, when she was a child, thought of simply as the river.

In the nineteen-twenties, dates had not much more importance to the people of the valley than they had to the river. Rociada was a clear pool into which the stream of time trickled and then stood still. Don José's three youngest children, Carmen, Consuelo, and Joséphine (Pepita), do not remember events of the period in sequence. For them, time spread out, taking on dimensions within which they wandered as they wandered within the actual area. The older children, Emilie, José, and Marie, already lightly meshed with the outside world, were beginning to feel the pull of linear, disappearing time. The little girls were a separate bunch, three little *mocas* running together. Don José was rather godlike, as a father should be — a fairly tall man, handsome, correct, slender, neat, with elegance about him. Doña Marguerite was not a person to be trifled with, but the little ones knew her more intimately than they did their father. She was small, very alive, intuitively chic. She managed to be at once perfectly French and perfectly Spanish, which is no small feat.

There was a balance between the ranch and the villages, and a balance between Don José and his wife. There have to be many balances within small groups in isolation, a tolerance and an interchange. One part does not merely support the other, but, like two slabs leaning against each other, both support, both are dependent. Don José was inclined to be severe. He had a big and busy home ranch to run, and between fifteen and twenty thousand head of sheep and some cattle to rotate safely between the summer ranges, in the high country near at hand, and the winter ranges, in the low country far to the south. He employed a throng of people — wranglers, sheepherders, cowpunchers, workmen — and, in the old New Mexico style, Don José drew these men, as Doña Marguerite did her servants, from the villages of Rociada and Upper Rociada. The people of the two villages received from them in return the multitude of services and attentions that traditionally they demanded of their *patrones.* Don José's relationship with the people was such that whenever some of his good horses were missing, he had only to tell Pascual, the official horse thief of Rociada, about it, indicating in a friendly way that he expected them back, and shortly they would appear again in his pasture.

From time to time Don José would fire a man, usually for good cause and usually, also, with some little irritation. Then there was not much for the man to do but fish, hunt in season, and cultivate his garden. The people were freeholders and free men; there was no peonage. A man could leave the valley and try his luck in Las Vegas or even farther away, in the arid, jostling world, but there were few who left Rociada if they could help it.

Soon enough the man's wife would come to Doña Marguerite with a tale of hungry children: they were out of flour, coffee, bacon; they had no more credit at Lobato's store in the village. One could not let the people go hungry. Doña Marguerite would get the wife supplies, taking them from the commissary or from her own kitchen. Simply to end the drain on her budget, she had to choose the moment to persuade her husband to forgive the man and hire him again.

Looking back across an abyss of change, my wife thinks of the village of Rociada first in terms of the weddings, and especially of Aurelia's wedding. Aurelia's father, Procopio Ruiz, was the most important man in the main village, so her wedding was a big affair. There was that, and then there was the business of Consuelo's and Carmen's hair, and that, in turn, was a symptom of their growing up. She was ten and Carmen twelve. They were growing up and becoming aware of grown-up matters, while Pepita, at eight, was still a baby. These things set Aurelia's wedding in Consuelo's mind.

The little girls all had black hair. Pepita's was long, with a marked natural curl at the ends. The older two wore their hair shorter, and it was, much to their regret, straight.

The afternoon before Aurelia's wedding, they gathered

pieces of paper and part of an old sheet, which they tore into strips, and that night they stayed up late putting each other's hair in curls. They felt freer to do this because the older children, who would have made fun of them, were away at boarding school or college. Their hair curled magnificently. When they came down to breakfast, Doña Marguerite said dryly that their heads were covered with corkscrews. They did not mind. They had looked at themselves in a mirror and were more than satisfied.

In the middle of the morning, they all got into the family automobile, a big Paige touring car, with their father at the wheel and their mother in the front seat beside him, to drive to the village. The Paige was an exhibition model with green leather upholstery, which Don José had seen and taken a fancy to in Denver. The three little girls, as it happened, all had new dresses. Carmen's was apple green, with a velvet sash reaching almost to her heels. She was very conscious of the dress and of her curls. Consuelo's dress was red, her favorite color, with a white yoke, which made her think of a nun, inspiring her briefly with saintly impulses. Pepita had a blue dress, with pink bows and embroidered butterflies. The car bumped and swayed in the ruts, kicking up a brown dust. The three little girls sat straight, their eyes quick and alert. They were quiet and correct from contained excitement and the sense of their finery.

The village was gathered at the Ruizes' house, on the plaza, back of the church. The house had a pitched tin roof, with the front slope carried out to make a shelter well beyond the front of the house and supported on round posts — a *portal.* Under the *portal* at the east end, the line of the sunlight had been traced as it fell along the wall about an hour before noon. At the west end, similarly, the dividing line between sun and shadow in early afternoon had been marked. Between these inward-sloping lines the wall had been calcimined a pale blue. Across the bottom ran a two-foot strip of bright-buff clay, full of gold sparkles, which make a sturdier coating than any lime wash. The wedding guests were standing around under the *portal* and just outside. Now that the *patrón* and *patrona* had arrived, the procession could form.

Most of the women wore shawls. The older women's shawls were black. Among Spanish-Americans, mourning lasts a long time, and as one grows older the deaths in one's far-reaching family crowd one upon another. The most modern of the younger women wore hats. The men were dressed in their best dark suits, their Sunday hats, smaller-brimmed than their everyday ones, and constraining collars. Some had neckties; some preferred the simple jewel-shine of a bright collar stud. Everyone was grave. The three little girls stood to one side, solemn, observant, and feeling a certain responsibility, because of their parents' role.

Then the procession started. First came Father Mueller, a very big bearded man, in his vestments. With his bulk, his rolling processional gait had a shiplike majesty. After him came the musicians, a violin and a guitar, playing cheerful polkas. Next were Don José and Doña Marguerite, as the bride's sponsors. That was their part in every wedding; without them, everyone would have felt that something was seriously wrong. Aurelia and her father followed them, then the groom and his companions, then the immediate families of both bride and groom. The three little girls came next after these, and behind them walked the rest of the village, along with people from Upper Rociada and Gascón, and from villages as far away as Sápello and Peñasco, beyond the walls of the valley.

The procession circled the plaza before it entered the church. The children wanted to be dignified, but polka music is not the best to walk sedately to, and they had to watch out for the unevennesses of the ground and not get their best slippers scuffed. They couldn't resist making some comment on the bride's white velvet gown, her veil and her wreath, and her satin slippers. Carmen asked Consuelo and Pepita if they had noticed the flash of the two gold fillings in Aurelia's front teeth when she smiled, and they had to fight off the giggles.

Consuelo found the service painfully long. The kneeling benches had been scrubbed with sand, and the sand had not been properly swept off. Her bare knees suffered. Sometimes Father Mueller enlivened Mass by saying the most outrageous things, but on this occasion he offered no entertainment. Finally, the service ended, and the procession returned to Ruiz's house, where the wedding guests formed a line, beginning at the *portal.*

It was some time before the girls' turn came to pass through the narrow doorway into the main room. Chairs lined the walls. In the middle was a table with refreshments on it. The bride and groom sat stiffly, side by side, at the back of the room. The happy couple were solemn to the point of misery. Consuelo thought that they looked as if they had taken convent vows of chastity and silence. The older people, sitting along the walls, did not look happy, either. Don José and Doña Marguerite, seated near the bride and groom, were solemn. Consuelo assumed that this was the way it was supposed to be, yet in view of all one heard beforehand, of all the plannings and anticipations, it always seemed strange. She wondered if her own wedding might be brighter.

The little girls spoke their formal congratulations and found seats. People continued to file in, greeting Don José and Doña Marguerite, as well as the bridal couple and their parents. The girls studied the table in the middle of the room, which was a shimmering lake of cakes with pink, green, and yellow icing, candies, nuts, fruits, pop, wine, and whiskey. The little girls sat for a long while in the severe silence, which they dared not break, trying not to squirm. They would happily have foregone the privilege of staying in the room along with relatives and honored elders, even though it meant an early turn at the refreshments. From outside the door they could hear a buzzing of talk and occasionally a young man's laugh.

In a strictly arranged order, the bride's parents invited people, one or a couple at a time, to "pass to the table." The guests took small helpings of this and that, and then sat down again and were ritually served chocolate. At last it was the little girls' turn, the three together, and before all the delicacies their polite self-control partly broke down. They had their laps full when the chocolate was brought to them.

The hot chocolate was deliciously right, with a marshmallow in each cup, and flavored with cinnamon. That drink, the *merienda,* is a minor capsule of history. The Spaniards learned its ceremonial use from the Aztecs and left the tradition of it even in these lost valleys. A later invasion added the marshmallow. No occasion such as a wedding would be complete without it.

The musicians started again; the company, except for the bride and groom, relaxed somewhat. The less important guests and the young people, who had been standing around outside, came in or were brought in, in small groups, to congratulate the bridal couple and to have refreshments. Some of the adults had begun to be warmed by wine or whiskey. Prohibition being in full force, the whiskey was water-clear local corn lightning; the wine was a sweet, heady red vintage from the neighborhood of Bernalillo, near Albuquerque. There were smiles here and there, a little gentle talk. After what seemed like ages to the children, the door to the next room was opened. In that room a long table had been set up; it was covered with a white tablecloth and was heavy with dishes. Again in turn the guests were invited to the wedding breakfast, a solid meal of everything good, from chili, beans, and mutton to Spanish pie, which is twice as much pastry as fruit, and bread pudding made with piñon nuts, raisins, wine, cheese, and cinnamon. There were bright bottles of pop on the table for those who did not take coffee.

It was a vast relief to the little girls to be told to go to the breakfast, to be released from stillness. They ate beyond desire, and left the table feeling slightly dizzy. It was proper for them to go outside now, so they walked away from the other guests and out under the *portal*, where they could draw deep breaths, take the sun on their faces, and wait for relief to set in.

After a few minutes Carmen, who had been standing by the front door, said, "Come on, if you want to see whether Aurelia cries." They hurried into the house after her just as the bride was going to her parents' bedroom with her mother and sisters. Carmen and Consuelo tagged after them, and Pepita was right behind. Sure enough, when Aurelia was sitting on the bed and her sisters had pulled off her slippers, she cried from the sheer easing of pain.

She had prayed and prayed, she said, that her father-in-law would get slippers to fit her when he bought her trousseau; all the time he was on his trip to Las Vegas she had prayed, but it had been no good. She might have known it was useless.

The slippers had been bought not to fit a foot of flesh and bone but to fit an idea. A bride is young, beautiful, Spanish, and her foot is tiny. The dainty, costly slippers would never be worn again. They were for that day, and it was necessary not that they fit Aurelia but that she should conform to them. Consuelo wondered if fathers-in-law liked to make brides cry. In her experience, the bride always did.

Aurelia was pale. She said there was no blood in her feet. The children chafed them until she felt better. She got her slippers back on and returned to the reception. The little girls stayed in the bedroom to admire the fine steamer trunk in which Aurelia's trousseau had come. Señora Ruiz's trunk, a solid affair of an older period, was in a central place against the wall in the same room, with a crocheted doily on top. Doña Marguerite had said once that wives cherished their trunks more than they did their husbands. Consuelo was sure her mother did not really think this. But the trunks were possessions for life; they were the repositories for all things of value — heirlooms, mementos, documents, savings.

Over Señora Ruiz's trunk hung her wedding picture. In the picture, she was standing partly beside, partly behind, the chair on which her husband sat, his legs crossed jauntily but his body rigid. Both of them wore fixed smiles. The artist who colored the picture had made the faces of the bride and groom so pink that they seemed to be blushing, and he had given Señor Ruiz blue eyes. Even so, Consuelo thought, it must have been a good likeness. Then it occurred to her that when Aurelia had her wedding picture taken, the photographer would probably paint out the gold spots in her teeth. Later, Consuelo learned that she had been right. She thought it was a pity.

The wedding guests sat through the balance of the afternoon inside the house, in shifts of silence and sparse talk, nibbling and sipping at the food and drink. Consuelo and her sisters again went outdoors to play, as best they could under the handicap of their best clothes. For a time, they held the blind woman, La Tulisa, in conversation, for the fascination of seeing whether a louse would appear on her hair. She had been born blind, and she was so dirty that Doña Marguerite would not allow her in the ranchhouse. At intervals, the children slipped indoors for refreshment.

At eight o'clock, everyone went to the dance hall for the wedding ball. How Aurelia managed it, the children did not know, but, in spite of her slippers, she seemed to be able to dance forever. Consuelo thought that she looked like a white moth miller. One looked forward to a wedding, and during it one had a sense of an event that had a special relationship to one's own future life, but the occasion itself became draggingly long. At the dance things picked up; there were movement, color, the smell of perfume and of people, the music. The little girls sat together, taking everything in. They noted with interest what men showed the effect of their drinks. There was an extra titillation in knowing that sometimes dances ended in fights, perhaps with knives or shooting, that possibly a fight would start before their father took them home, or that at least they might see the *bastonero* (the bouncer) put out a drunk.

Don José drove them home at nine. The children were exhausted enough to go willingly to bed. Consuelo thought that it had been a good wedding and a wonderful day. Her hair was straightening out again; she knew sadly that in another day it would be as straight as ever. Neither Aurelia's trunk nor Señora Ruiz's compared with her mother's, which had been brought from Mexico and was magnificent, of tan leather, brass studded, with all sorts of divided trays inside. That was the kind of trunk Consuelo wanted to have.

That is, if she got married. It might be better to be a

nun. You might marry, and then there might be a war, and your husband might be killed, like Tomás Romero, from Upper Rociada, in the World War. The girls had been reading stories about wars, old ones, and Consuelo noticed that women sent their husbands to the wars. If you did not marry, you would not have to send a man, and so he would not be killed. It might be better not to have either a husband or a trunk, and enter a convent and be holy.

If she did get married, she hoped that she might have a little more fun at her wedding. She knew that, among people like her parents, things were often done differently from the way that was customary in the village; perhaps their weddings were not so solemn. Then, sleepily, she remembered that all her family had small feet; her mother's were tiny. At least, if she did get married, the chances were that her slippers would fit her, and her father-in-law would not be able to make her cry.

Consuelo's wedding was a small one, in Manhattan. She wore a smart going-away dress and black pumps, which she had selected for herself. The reception, in a small apartment on Murray Hill, was brightly gay with champagne. The groom gave her an overnight case with her initials on it. Of all the great clan of the Bacas, only her sister Carmen was present.

II

A Voice in Mid-August

THE SUMMER that Pino Baca, my brother-in-law, was thirteen, he was troubled by loneliness. It was also that summer that his father gave him the Remington .22. After nine months of exile in an Eastern boarding school, Pino came home in June. The First World War had already begun, but it was still merely "the war in Europe." It in no way disturbed the blissful eternity of a long vacation at Rociada.

There were open, rich pasture lands over which one could ride fast with a slack rein. Rapid streams full of unsophisticated trout came out of the side canyons and wound through the pastures in the main valley to join the rushing Río Manuelitas. On all sides, the mountain slopes led away and upward, inviting exploration and hunting; behind the immediately enclosing heights were more valleys and then higher peaks, full of mystery and challenge. In the rough forested country and in the intricate system of valleys of the home area and beyond the ridges, Pino's father grazed his cattle and sheep. In the wide horse pasture was a *caballada* of a hundred and fifty horses. The villages which lay within the boundaries of the ranch, and Gascón, which Pino could reach in about an hour and a half on horseback, had their full share of eccentric and interesting characters. One would have said that a boy who had the freedom of all the land dominated by Don José's Wineglass-2 brand and of all the country into which that land led had just about everything a boy could ask for. It seems strange, on the face of it, that Don José Baca's only son — the princeling, as it were, of his domain — should have found any cause for discontent.

At the beginning of summer, Pino had the wonderful feeling that summer would never end. School remained in his mind only to the extent that, recurrently, the assurance of being not there but back at Rociada caused floods of conscious happiness to course through his system. Even so, he had periods when he felt at a loss. Not all the time but too often he needed, and did not have, a companion.

Pino had five sisters. Five sisters is a load for any boy. One of them, Emilie, was older than he; Pino had to be watchful and resistant or he would find her assuming authority over him. The four others, ranging from eleven down to a cradle baby, were, to his mind, just plain useless. Girls as a class and of a reasonable age he was beginning to find not entirely uninteresting, but sisters were a headache.

He got on well with his father's sheepherders, wranglers, and cowpunchers. They were almost all Rociada people;

their families and his had lived side by side for two generations, ranch and villages forming one community. The men accepted Pino naturally, but, after all, they were grownups.

That year, while Pino was away, a newcomer had been added to the staff, Cayetano the Mexican, whom the others often spoke of as El Chihuahueño, although he came not from Chihuahua but from the distant tropics of Veracruz. Cayetano was an ex-revolutionary. He had impressive bushy, drooping mustaches; he was short and very dark. He had ridden with Varela, who rose against Porfirio Díaz even before Madero led his revolution; then Varela threw in with Madero and was shot when Huerta took over. Cayetano fled to the States, and wound up that spring working for Don José. He turned out to be, as Señor Juan, the *mayordomo*, remarked, "*tan payaso como nosotros*" ("just as much a hick as any of us"). For a time, he fascinated Pino with his tales of warfare, but eventually they palled on the boy, as they had on the men, and Pino ceased listening to him.

In the three villages there were plenty of boys. Their usefulness as companions was limited; up to a point they served, and then they failed. Pino was not especially conscious of the difference in their manner of speech and he was no snob, but that difference typified deeper, more important separations that prevented true companionship. Pino, like his father, was bilingual. He spoke an English free of the localisms and dialect elements of the ordinary Anglo-American cowpuncher's or rancher's; similarly, his Spanish was of the correct Latin-American variety, distinctly different from his neighbor's archaic seventeenth-century speech. Also, the beginnings of maturity and the influence of his year at boarding school had made Pino less naïve in his relations with people. All in all, he was thrown a good deal upon himself, and there were times when being just with himself left him incomplete.

It was by no means always up to the boy to figure out what to do with his time. His father assigned him a fair amount of responsible work, and paid him for it. Since these assignments kept him out-of-doors, involved activities at which he wanted to excel, and usually required riding, Pino did not mind them, although he would have felt easier had his father's standards been less exacting. Don José's idea of what his son's education should embrace covered a lot of territory. The boy should have a good general education, with Latin, and a sound grounding in the Catholic faith. He should speak correct English and Spanish, and know some French. He should be familiar with the English classics and enjoy the use of books. He should be able to ride, shoot, rope, train horses, and manage sheep and cattle at least as well as any of the men who would someday work under him, and he should master the many aspects, commercial and agricultural, of running a great ranch. Along with this knowledge and these arts, he must have the manner and manners of a gentleman, according to both the English and the Spanish standards. Don José's ambition for his son was saved from unreasonableness by the fact that he himself had all these accomplishments.

For a while that summer Pino was foreman of a fence-repairing crew, with four workmen under him. One of the men, Epifanio Gutiérrez, was elderly, gray-haired, and experienced. Don José considered that he would offset any weaknesses of extreme youth in his foreman. Epifanio and Pino often varied the monotony of fencing by playing a game of mumblety-peg, with a can of Prince Albert tobacco as stake. As Epifanio won two times out of three, the boy pretty well kept him in tobacco, and this, in turn, presented problems.

Pino was saving his earnings, or trying to save them, to buy a wonderful knife that Lobato, who ran the store, was holding for him. The knife had three blades, a can opener, a screwdriver, a gimlet, and a hook for taking stones out of horses' hoofs. The cost of the Prince Albert cut into his savings. And then, obviously, he could not be always buying tobacco, whether from Lobato or from his father's commissary, without causing awkward questions to be asked. His father would approve neither of the mumblety-peg during working hours nor of the betting. Pino had to steal the cans from the commissary and slip money into the till when no one was looking. It was a complicated procedure, but it had its sporting aspects.

In August, Don José gave him the Remington .22. It was a reward for a good first year at boarding school, and compensation for that exile. It was a repeater, chambered for long cartridges, and better than any gun Pino had been allowed to use theretofore. It had a good balance and solid weight, so it held steady. With this weapon and a horse, the half-understood uneasiness of solitary expeditions vanished.

One day, while the rifle was still a fresh delight, Pino's horse developed a saddle gall. Señor Juan showed it to Don José with disapproval, and Pino's father told the boy simply that he couldn't ride his horse or any of the others until his animal was cured. Don José was generous — he had given Pino a rifle, and the following summer he gave him a Model T — but no fault in his son was let pass unpunished.

The temporary loss of the use of the horse, combined with the knowledge that his father was displeased and considered him negligent, depressed Pino. That afternoon, he set out on foot with his rifle. He felt vaguely resentful and abused, although he knew that saddle galls are caused by carelessness. He wanted to be alone; he wanted to lose himself. He knew that he lacked something, but he didn't know what. He needed someone who matched him, with whom he could talk.

The afternoon was hot and still. Stopping on the wooden bridge over the river, behind the stillness he thought he heard a voice. Or was it a voice? He looked up to the mountains east and west of the valley; he looked at the bright blue sky where it met the bald rounded peak of El Ermitaño, from which the last snow was gone. He smelled the hot sun on ripe grass, and remembered that as he was leaving the house he had heard the clackety sound of the mowing machines in the meadow downriver and the voice of a man guiding a team. He knew suddenly what he had just heard behind the sunlight and the silence: it was September, autumn, coming.

At that moment the long vacation ceased to be endless.

Mid-September would come, and he would leave Rociada for another nine endless months, another whole lifetime. School was real once more, menacing him from halfway across America. He saw that the sprinkling of wild yellow blooms, sunflowers and chamiso, had increased greatly in the past few days. The smell of the grass was a late smell, different from that of June; the stalks were drying, ready for cutting. Soon, he knew, he would find asters. He studied the mountain slopes and saw with relief that as yet there was no sign of the aspen or the oak brush turning.

He thrust the sense of hurrying time away from him. For a few weeks yet he would generally be successful in closing off the foreknowledge of ending and of school; at moments he would really forget about it. Now, with that realization pushed away for the first time, he was violently restless.

He tried hunting gophers. He was a good shot, but gophers are wary; the sport was not much fun. He wandered, seeking targets. He needed the satisfaction and minor violence of bullets striking their marks. He made a wide circle from north of the ranchhouse westward, then went back across the river, west and south between the ranch and the main village, then easterly, shooting at, in turn, a rabbit, a tree stump, a tobacco can thrown away long ago and faded from scarlet to dull rose. Finally, stalking and taking cover, he made his way through the orchard, coming out not far from the miscellaneous sheds beyond the barns.

He scouted the outbuildings, seeing no one. Someone

had been washing his father's carriage, the best one, of bright varnished wood, with the wheels, spokes, and whiffletrees picked out with lines of deep blue and the seats upholstered in heavy brown leather. The carriage was in a semi-retired status, Don José having taken to motorcars, but it was still well cared for, kept bright, and occasionally put to use. This afternoon, it had been pulled out, washed, and left standing in the open. Pino reflected that it ought to be put back under protection from sun and dust. He noticed how the sunlight gleamed on the varnish. On the side that enclosed one end of the front seat, a large knot, around which the grain swirled, stood out and made a small, distant, clear bull's-eye.

He drew a bead on the knot, pretending. It showed up sharply defined in his rear sight; the bead of the front sight, low in the notch, covered its lower half. Without intending to, without volition, he squeezed the trigger and the rifle cracked. Instantly, horror seized him. Now he *was* in trouble.. Hiding the gun behind a tree, he went forward, hoping against hope that he had made a wild miss, watchful lest anyone appear to witness his actions. The bullet had plugged the knot neatly, loosening it, and glancing upward, dragged a long scar across the leather of the seat. He had made the shot of his life. Turning, he ran back to the shelter of the orchard, and there he lay flat in the long grass, wondering what to do. Punishment would be inescapable and painfully adequate.

Someone moved near the barn over to the far right. It was Cayetano, who now strolled diagonally toward the orchard and leaned against a shed, in the shade, to roll a cigarette. Cayetano didn't work steadily unless he was watched. Pino studied him. He really was *payaso;* he was curiously simple for a man with so adventurous a past. Desperate inspiration came to the boy.

He emptied his rifle quietly. With his pocketknife, he pried the bullet out of a cartridge and stuffed the end with a scrap of paper he found in his pocket. He inserted the homemade blank directly into the chamber. He picked up the other cartridges, rose, and sauntered over to Cayetano, who, as he drew near, looked quickly over his shoulder. You could see the knot from there, but you couldn't see the bullet hole, or that the knot had been loosened.

"*Buenas tardes, Cayetano,*" Pino said politely.

"*Buenas tardes, hijo.*" Old training in Mexico made Cayetano address his *patrón*'s son somewhat more courteously than the native North American workmen did, but he refrained from addressing a thirteen-year-old boy as *Don.*

Pino made idle talk. The Mexican's eyes studied the rifle. He asked about it. Pino saw that he was approaching the bait and encouraged Cayetano to talk of his own skill with rifles, of the weapons he had caried in battle, and so to spacious, happily unverifiable tales of his marksmanship. As the Mexican talked of those days and drew upon the brilliance of distance and imagination, his dark eyes brightened, his face became animated.

"Between the eyes, man — here, *en punto* — at forty yards, and all I had to sight on was the gleam of his eyeballs in the light of the stars."

The boy said that had been good luck. The Mexican said no, it was constant practice and the true domination of one's arm. They talked on, half arguing, Pino skeptical, Cayetano insisting.

"Here, if you're so expert," Pino said. "I bet you two reals I know a target equally big that you can't hit at half the distance, and in the light of day."

"Where is it? Show me."

"Over here," Pino said. He led Cayetano to a point between the carriage and where he had stood in the orchard. "Have you two reals?"

The Mexican felt in his pocket and brought out a quarter. "Here, see." His manner was offended. "And you?"

"Here." Pino brought out his own quarter, glanced at it, thinking of the knife in Lobato's store, and then said quickly, "You bet?"

"Surely. How not? Show me the target."

Pino put the rifle into Cayetano's hands. "I bet you two reals you can't hit that knot there. Very well I know you can't."

Cayetano did not answer. He was angry. He threw up the rifle, aimed, and fired. The report was of a blank cartridge, but Cayetano didn't notice.

Pino said, "Let's go to see." They walked up to the carriage. "You win," Pino said. "What a shot! Here you are." He handed over his quarter.

"*Ay,* look what I've done!" Cayetano cried out. "Look you that which you have made me do!"

"Oooh! That my papa will be angry! You'd better go and tell him."

"No, that you tell him. Please!" Cayetano begged. "That you say a word for me — that I was not thinking, that I did not mean . . . "

Pino could not well refuse, although he would have preferred to stay completely out of the affair. That evening, he explained to his father that he had never dreamed the Mexican would actually shoot at the carriage; he hadn't thought anyone could be as dumb as that. He made his bet sound casual, as if it had been purely rhetorical. He could see that his father was displeased again, and baffled, as though he felt that there was more here than showed on the surface but did not know where to look for it.

Don José went out to the bunkhouse and had a talk with Cayetano. The man was a really fine *vaquero,* too useful to fire even for an imbecility, as long as it had nothing to do with his performance of his work. The *patrón* left him humble, penitent, and full of admiration for a magnificent dressing-down. The following day, Cayetano thanked the boy profusely for having spoken in his behalf and saved his job.

The incident was closed, but Pino still felt uneasy, not because of the device by which he had got himself out of trouble and not because he had involved Cayetano, for nothing serious had happened to Cayetano. It was Cayetano's being so grateful on such false grounds that disturbed the boy. It took him till the end of the vacation to figure out what to do. On the morning of the fifteenth of September, the day before he was to leave Rociada, he bought the knife, at last. As a possession he esteemed it second only to the rifle, and it had the advantage that it could go with him to school. That night, lying in bed, he remembered that the sixteenth of September was the Mexican equivalent of the Fourth of July, and that Cayetano had permission to celebrate. He would probably be drunk by noon and spend the rest of the day pleasantly sleeping it off in the orchard.

Before breakfast on the fatal day of departure, Pino sought him out. He spoke of the occasion, said that he knew Cayetano must think with longing of his home on this day, and added some graceful words about sister republics, lifted from an editorial in the Santa Fe Spanish-language paper, *El Nuevo Mexicano*. Then he presented Cayetano with the knife. Cayetano was so overwhelmed that he lifted his hat and addressed the boy as Don Pino.

Pino left for school most unwillingly but with a clear conscience. In mid-November, his mother wrote him that Cayetano had quit the ranch in disgust when he learned that the snow and cold that had come upon them would continue into April.

The carriage slept in its shed. The injury it had received was forgotten. In time, the leather became dry and cracked, and the same year that Don José bought the Paige touring car, the carriage was sold.

III

The Loss of a Hero

THERE IS a drawn-out excitement in the long-continued fast travel of a pack train, even though the rate at which it moves is still far slower than that which unencumbered horsemen would maintain. For Pino, sixteen years old, riding at the head of what he allowed himself to think of as his outfit, this excitement was heightened by the sense of command and responsibility, and by a difference between this trip and any other he had made.

On his gray horse, he led the way through the signless uniformity of a wide aspen grove, holding a steady fox trot, as the pack train had been doing almost continuously for the past three hours. He wore a gray Stetson, a wine-red shirt of fine flannel set off by a blue silk scarf, levis, hand-stitched boots, and spurs. He rode standing in the stirrups, his weight thrown forward and resting on his hands, which were crossed over the horse's neck just in front of the saddle, with the reins passing over his left thumb and under the palm of his hand. He had a light rifle in a scabbard under his leg.

Behind him followed four snugly packed, neat-stepping mules. Pascual Orozco rode at the rear, keeping the mules to their pace with the threat, and occasionally the sting, of the end of his lariat. In theory, he was Pino's helper, but Pino knew perfectly well that his own command of the outfit, at least so long as it was in motion, was a polite fiction. This day, Pino's father had put him in charge of a mission to rush supplies to one of his sheep camps, and the expedition was unusual in more than the element of haste.

The camp was not in Don José's usual summer range, which sprawled over the central portion of the Sangre de Cristo Mountains in northern New Mexico, but on a tract he had leased along Cow Creek, farther west, on the slopes leading to the Pecos River. There he was holding a couple of thousand sheep for which, in a dry year, he lacked room elsewhere. A main ridge of the mountains separated the home ranch at Rociada from the camp. The herders there had sent word that they would be out of grub by evening. Señor Juan, the Bacas' *mayordomo,* as a rule so efficient, had slipped up.

The usual way of going by a roundabout, rough trail made this trip at best a long, slow day's ride for a pack train. It was nearly noon when word of the difficulty reached Rociada. Don José calculated that if he did not get supplies of some sort to Cow Creek before the sun went down — and this was not possible by the known trails — the men would be saddling up and riding down toward Pecos to get themselves fed by friends and relatives, leaving the flock untended, at the mercy of wild animals and the innate idiocy of sheep. So he called in Pascual Orozco, the local horse thief.

Before telling about what happened on this ride, I must describe Pascual. I attempt this with some hesitation. Pino has told me about him at length, and I have discussed him with Doña Marguerite, with my wife, and with other members of the Baca family. Their descriptions tally; there is no question of the facts, and I will not alter them merely to insure belief. The trouble is that Pascual at the height of his career, before he tainted the antique purity of horse-thieving with the mechanized commerce of bootlegging, sounds like something out of pulp fiction. He was tall. His dark hair had coppery glints in it, and the Western-style mustache that framed his firm, cruel mouth was definitely red. His eyes were black, and when he was angry they seemed to be armed. His skin was dark from years and years of sun and wind — not from any apparent Indian inheritance. He was aquiline, and handsome. He affected black clothing of considerable elegance, partly for dramatic effect and partly because it was a good color for his night operations.

Pascual could have been a prosperous local citizen. Leaving aside the Bacas, who reckoned their land by the square mile rather than by the acre, he was one of the large landowners of the district, with a hundred and fifty acres, much of it under ditch. Farming did not interest him; he left that to his two younger brothers — peaceable family men of a temperament to walk behind a plow. Horses were what he cared for and horses he dealt in, in his own special fashion.

As a usual thing, he dropped down into the lowlands south of Las Vegas to pick out a string, which he would run up into the mountains to hidden narrow-mouthed valleys known only to him. In due course, their brands being expertly altered, he would take the string north into Colorado, and on through the defiles and hidden places of the Rockies, until he reached Wyoming, where he sold the horses off. After an interlude of high life at Cheyenne, Laramie, or Denver, he would work his way south, picking up another string as he came along, for sale in central New Mexico. Thus he maintained the balance of trade. Other men lifted horses in that country at that time, but from Trinidad to Pecos, from Taos to Wagon Mound, those who knew about this subject considered Pascual in a class by himself. In his home territory of Rociada, he was *the* horse thief, and no one dreamed of competing with him.

This day, he was riding his Apalousian, a horse he had purchased in open trade; he could always show clear title to any animal he kept in his own pasture. The horse stood a shade over fifteen hands, moved beautifully, and was, as is common with that breed, a roan with a dramatic irregular white splotch covering most of its hindquarters. Pascual was wearing an expensive black stetson, a black-and-white checked flannel shirt, black boots stitched with red and green, and iron pants. Iron pants are of fine, hard wool, cut snug in the seat and upper legs for riding. From a little distance, the material suggests that of cutaway trousers, but the paired white pin stripes are a trifle more pronounced against the black background. This sober ensemble was relieved by a maroon silk scarf, and by Pascual's hardware.

His spurs were large-roweled, silver-mounted, made in Mexico. At his waist he wore a cartridge belt, from which his revolver hung in its holster. The cartridge belt was ordinary, decorative only in the gleam of brass shell ends in the loops. His holster, made to order in Mexico, was embroidered with the Mexican eagle. The gun in it was a Colt .45 with an eleven-inch barrel and a mother-of-pearl handle. In the handle was set a small but genuine diamond.

As the outfit flowed along between the aspens, Pascual called to the boy in the lead, in Spanish, "Eye peeled for an aspen where there is *Yo amo a Anita* carved inside a heart. At the right. There, take the right."

Pino watched, saw the inscription made by some lonesome sheepherder, and turned. Pascual called, "Seest thou the deer run? Take it to the left."

For an instant, Pino was afraid he wouldn't see the run; then his eye caught the difference between it and dozens of almost identical aisles, and he followed it.

It had been like that all along. Pino, from a whole boyhood of ranging the mountains, knew the trails and the dim trails. He knew three feasible ways of reaching Cow Creek from Rociada. But Pascual knew the routes without trails. He knew how the naturally open swales and *cañadas* ran. He knew the hidden breaks in the cliffs, and how one could reach the saddles in the high ridges that were supposed to be inaccessible. He knew where a short scramble up a rockslide led to a cleft that cut off miles. He was master of the open going between the tall stems of the evergreen forests, and where other men, out of sight of the sun, would go off course little by little until they became lost, he had a thousand insignificant landmarks by which he found his way. Pino knew how to make good time, but Pascual held his own horse and the mules before him to a steady speed that gave the boy a sense of breathless, remorseless hurry.

From the moment they climbed out of Rociada valley, Pascual had guided the train on a crow-flight routing of his own, taking the rear in order to maintain the pace. The directions had followed one upon another: "Go by that peeled aspen." "See that red cliff above the trees? Head straight for that." "When thou seest a horse's skull under a mountain mahogany, give to the left." The instructions (calling often for quick, fine observation), the pace, and the boy's fear that he would go by that skull, not see the deer run, combined to build up in Pino a more and more excited tension.

This, the boy thought with a thrill, was how Pascual traveled with his stolen horses. Pascual was revealing to him a corner of his secret. It was a demonstration of trust in him and of friendship, as well as of deference to his father — one of the very few men toward whom Pascual showed respect.

As he rode, the boy thought of the scope of Pascual's operations — the distances, the skill, and the danger. His heart uplifted, he dreamed of the night passages, not with mules but with a string of fast-trotting horses, until another shouted instruction brought him back to reality and he was acutely attentive again, lest he make a slip in Pascual's presence. Suddenly Pino saw, stretching across the lower end of a long, shallow, open depression, the treacherous brilliant green of a *ciénaga,* a turf-covered bog. He raised his left hand, ready to draw rein. Pascual shouted, "*Dale! Dale!* Give it! On the run, man!" As he spoke, he let out more of the end of his lariat and swung it over his head; then he whooped at the mules.

Pino settled himself in the saddle, plied his spurs, and whipped his horse with the long ends of his reins. His horse went into a lope, then a high lope, as it reached the green covering. It was not going fast enough; it began to flounder. Pino's instinct was to swing it around before it bogged. The mules slowed their pace, and bunched up, hesitating at the edge of the bog.

Pascual seemed to become four or five men. He was up within reach of the boy, ahead of the mules, shouting "Give it!" and swinging his lariat. The rope's end caught boy and horse impartially, galvanizing both. Pino lashed with the rein ends. The horse leaped forward, floundered once more, gained speed, and went across at a dead run. By then Pascual was behind the mules again, and brought them over in a racing bunch. It was necessary after that to get down and check the packs, to make sure that the burst of speed had not loosened them. Pino was glad of the respite, and it seemed to him that the only man greater than Pascual in all the world was his father.

It did not occur to him then or later that there was any call for Pascual, theoretically of inferior station and at the moment his father's employee, to apologize for having caught him a number of painful licks, intentionally or unintentionally. When you have not only just witnessed but taken part in a miracle, you do not object if in the course of it the miracle-worker caused you some slight physical discomfort.

The pack train reached the camp early enough to enable the men to have their supper at the usual time, and that day's ride (they returned more at leisure, by a conventional route) fortified Pino's hero worship of Pascual, to which everything about the man contributed. He was dangerous. Those who crossed him had their fence cut or their animals lamed, or woke in the night to find their barns afire. He was a man of some mystery — a bachelor (in itself an anomaly in that region) living in a house which, from the outside, looked deserted and neglected. The people of Rociada, Upper Rociada, and Gascón were much given to visiting among themselves and at the ranch, but very few had ever been inside Pascual's house, the blinds of which were always drawn.

He was a far-ranger, not traveled in the sense that Pino's parents were but still knowledgeable about many cities outside the mountains. A man of his parts required more elaborate entertainment than Rociada could provide. From time to time, he took his pleasure with elegance in Las Vegas, which, in the days just before prohibition, was an opulent, well-equipped lively city. Sometimes Pascual went farther abroad. He dropped casual remarks about the sights and diversions of Denver and Cheyenne, of El Paso, and of the explosive little adobe town of Ciudad Juárez across the border — remarks calculated to fascinate a boy in his teens.

With women he was both effective and unscrupulous (Doña Marguerite once remarked that he ruined every woman who let herself be friendly with him) — a trait that only added to his glamour in Pino's eyes. Rociada born and bred, to that place Pascual always, like almost all of Rociada's children, returned.

As I have said, Pascual showed deference to Don José; he also worked for Don José from time to time, although he did not particularly need the pay. Possibly it pleased him to be needed by the great house. None of Don José's children feels that any explanation of this attitude of respect is necessary, nor does Doña Marguerite, which is to me an impressive indication of the kind of man Don José was. As for Doña Marguerite, she had no use for Pascual at all, and he avoided her.

He ran a small bunch of cattle, partly because it was work that appealed to him, partly as a cover for his many unexplained absences. From time to time, during dry spells, Don José let him throw the cattle in with his own herd, on the lower meadowlands. Early in Pascual's career, the matter of the ranch's relationship to him was settled smoothly. Don José had a beautiful young blooded mare that Pascual desired greatly to buy. When it became clear that the *patrón* would not sell, the mare, as might have been expected, disappeared from the horse pasture where she had been turned loose. The theft was probably an experiment, a testing. It was reported on a Tuesday evening. Wednesday morning, Don José sent for Pascual. No one else was present at the interview between them. Don José was older than Pascual, and taller, and he had the gift of being quietly forceful without apparent emphasis. The grand manner was his by nature. He told Pascual that his mare was missing from the pasture and that the fence was not down anywhere. As Pascual knew, he valued the animal highly. He hoped that Pascual would help find her, and he was confident that however she got out, she would return by the same means, not later than Friday morning.

That was all there was to it. The mare was in the pasture Friday morning. I have never heard of any other human being to whom Pascual deferred.

Pascual took the jobs that appealed to him. He was a fine teamster, and proud of his ability to push a team and loaded wagon over the bad mountain roads in snow or deep mud. In those days, not only the cart track that served as a road between Rociada and Sápello, the village at the gateway to the high mountain country, but the state road from there to Las Vegas, the metropolis on the railroad, frequently became impassable to automobiles. At such times, Pascual was the man who could be counted on to get the ranch's supplies through, behind two or four horses, so he handled most of Don José's heavy trucking for him. He liked work with cattle and horses but not with sheep. He was called in on occasions when some interloper, some comparative amateur, had the effrontery to steal one of the Baca horses. Pascual followed up those cases with vigor and success, considering the stealing of a horse within his own home district a personal insult. While Pascual was doing these occasional jobs for the ranch, Pino had come in contact with him and had won his friendship.

Various lesser incidents than the one of the *ciénaga* and the cross-country ride increased the boy's admiration. One time, Pino was walking with Pascual on the edge of the woods. Pino was carrying his .22 rifle. He spotted a grouse in a tree, aimed hastily, fired, and missed. Before the grouse could take flight, Pascual killed it neatly with a flung stone. The acts of stooping, picking up the stone, straightening, and throwing were performed as a single motion almost too swift to follow. The mixture of quick action, skill, and deadliness was characteristic.

Pino still was spending nine months of each year at a boarding school deep in the East. As he was the only boy there who had roped, punched cattle, and ridden bucking horses, he commanded a ready audience, which enabled him to assuage some part of his homesickness with tales of Rociada. He had learned early to temper the truth, both plain and adorned, in such a way as to avoid incredulity or plain incomprehension. Pascual symbolized to him an important aspect of his homeland, but at school he never mentioned him; he could see no way to tell about his idol without having him rejected as a tall tale.

Pino superimposed upon the average American boy's belief that he is already a man the Spanish necessity of being and proving himself one. Pascual's stature became progressively greater in Pino's eyes. The harshest aspect of the man's character — even his vices — fascinated the boy, until Pascual himself destroyed it all with a single cast of a lariat.

Don José had given Pino the Model T when he was

fourteen. He became the family courier for those errands best performed in a car, the errands reaching to more distant places as he grew older. When he was seventeen, a year after his ride to Cow Creek, he was sent to Las Vegas occasionally, and to Sápello more times than suited his convenience. Sápello, as I have said, was the gateway to the Rociada country, and to home-staying villagers it seemed a place well worth visiting. The priest lived there; it had two stores and a regular bar, as well as a dance hall. The main village of Rociada, in contrast, had neither priest nor bar, and only one store. To Pino with his knowledge of the outside world, Sápello was just another village, with no attractions, and set in unattractive country. A trip there was simply an interruption of more interesting activities.

That summer, too, there was a new annoyance on the road. A family from outside had taken up an old farm on the road to Sápello, not far from Peñasco. It is Pino's impression that the family were Anglo-Americans of some kind; he remembers a towheaded boy. If they were, that would help explain the trick that Pascual played. This family brought with them some dogs as neglected and various as any that drifted about the houses of the natives. They were a source of constant irritation because they rushed wildly at cars — not just barking and running alongside but surrounding the car and apparently trying to board it. At that point on that rutted, washed-out road, in the cars of 1918, one drove between ten and twelve miles an hour; the dogs hung on long, and Pino was often forced half off the road in order to avoid them. Their leader, a big dog whose principal element was collie, was especially persistent, fierce, and annoying.

One day when Pascual was at the ranch, Doña Marguerite asked Pino to drive to Sápello with a message for the priest. Pascual said that he had business there, too, and the boy gladly offered him a ride. When they had left the ranchhouse, Pascual said, "Bring me a lariat — any old one. I'm going to show thee how one can teach good customs to those dogs the other side of Peñasco."

Pino brought him an old rope. Pascual tied the dally end to the back spring, brought the rope around to the right-hand door, and got in, with the rest of it coiled in his hand.

"What goest thou to do?

"Thou wilt see," Pascual said.

As it was a fine, sunny day, they drove with the top down. In due course, they reached Peñasco, a scattering of farms that by a quality of conjunction, of being closer together than other mountain farms, created the sense of a place that deserved a name. When they were past it, Pascual said, "Now, when we go by the ranch of the curs, keep traveling, follow straight, and when I say 'Give it,' *give* it."

They went by the farm; the dogs rushed out. Pino held the car steady at about twelve miles an hour. Pascual leaned out the door, rope in hand. The dog that was part collie made one of his snarling leaps at the car, and Pascual flipped the loop neatly over his head.

"Dale!"

Without thinking, Pino pulled down the throttle. The

car leaped to twenty miles an hour, jarring his backbone. He heard a strange, very short, strangled scream and felt a jerk as the rope snapped tight behind them. The other dogs howled and scattered. He threw the throttle up, but Pascual said, "Give it, man! Now begins the dance."

Pino drove on. This was the thing inside Pascual. You knew he was deadly, and that fascinated you, but you had never dreamed what it would be like to have him let you see it. Pino was afraid, and he was also ashamed to stop or protest. Pascual sat placidly, not even looking back. Behind them, the dog bumped and dragged. Pino drove as fast as he could, and the animal followed at the end of the rope; it stayed on, he thought, forever, following the car. Then the jerking stopped.

Pascual said, "Stand thyself. There's no grace in dragging that rope." Pino stopped.

Pascual got out and went to the back of the car. Pino would not turn his head, but in the rearview mirror he saw Pascual stand for a moment looking down the road. Then he untied the empty lariat, coiled it, and got in. The honda and about a foot of the rope nearest it showed traces of hair and blood.

"Its head separated itself," Pascual said informatively.

The boy drew in an unsteady breath. He was José Baca, son of José Baca; he would not be sick, he would keep a still face. He drove on to Sápello. Pino's business with the priest was brief; Pascual had some complicated negotiations in hand, so Pino drove home alone.

Not until several years later did Pino tell anyone what had happened. It was a thing he could not bring himself to describe. He tried to bury the sharp memory of the dog's choked cry, and the visual images; he had to deal, also, for a month or so, with a recurrent, definite sense of loss. At moments when he thought of the horse thief, or when he met him, first would come the old familiar admiration, then the remembering. And if Pascual was physically present, Pino would assume the graceful politeness that is the ancient Spanish mask. At this time Pascual stopped addressing him as "thou."

IV

God in the Mountains

AS A CHILD my wife Consuelo enjoyed an active religious life, which received special coloration from the milieu in which she grew up. I say "enjoyed" because, even more than the rest of the Bacas, she and the two sisters nearest her in age, Carmen and Pepita, never failed to extract full value from any emotional situation, and their religion had a content of emotion and incident beyond the average even for Spanish Catholicism. It was this sense of the dramatic that led them to conclude, when Consuelo was seven and their much admired brother Pino was eighteen, that the wrath of God was sure to be visited upon him.

Rociada is in a country where the devout will find the hand of God continually manifest, in wild thunderstorms and a ferocity of lightning, in heavy, swirling blizzards, in occasional forest fires, and perhaps most truly in the way the face of the land eternally changes, from morning to afternoon to night, from season to season, from fair day to foul.

In extreme youth the three youngest sisters were most deeply impressed by the thunderstorms. The terrific roll and echo of the thunder, the blinding flashes coming ever nearer, the rush and force of the wall of rain on the roof and on windows that had turned into cataracts seen inside out, were high and terrifying drama. They responded to it wholeheartedly, strengthened in this by the fact that their mother herself was distinctly frightened by lightning.

When their father was home, Doña Marguerite took the storms relatively calmly and the girls, in their turn, felt protected. They did not argue that their father could turn back the wrath of God if once God determined to wipe them out, but they were sure that He would never want to strike down Don José, and that God would at least listen to him if he should put up an argument as to the fate of others.

When Don José was away, which happened often enough in the course of his management of the ranch, as when the sheep and cattle were moving between summer and winter ranges, at lambing time, and during the fall sales, as well as in the course of his political activities, things were different. Then, when nature decided to cut loose, most especially at night, when the mountains boomed and roared, the water pounded on the house, and black windows flashed blinding white at intervals, they fully expected their end. The three of them would run to their mother's room, where they would find her already up and lighting the candles on the little altar. They would kneel as close to her as they could, praying industriously to the image of the Blessed Virgin and counting over and repenting their sins, until at last God let the storm roll away to other valleys and the noise on the roof, steadier and more insistent than drumming, dwindled to a gentle patter.

They had two cousins about their age who lived in Las Vegas. Perhaps because they had a certain city sophistication, these girls showed a courage in the face of storms which the little Bacas greatly admired. When the lightning started, they did not go to their mother, but lighted candles on an altar they had in their own room, got in between two feather puffs for insulation, pulled the upper one over their heads and toughed it out. This was bravery; it was also much less fun.

Pino, to the extent that he allowed himself to be conscious of his youngest sisters' fear of storms, looked on it with disgust. In his eighteenth year they found him irritating in many ways, for being in his last winter at boarding school, with college looming before him, when he was at home he played the grown man industriously, expected a good deal of service from the children, and from time to time took it upon himself to correct them. They thought he was getting too big for his boots and they decided that, among other failings, he was falling off badly in his religion.

In fact he was not, but, perhaps in rebellion against the enforced, continuous piety of school, he did assume a young irreverence at times. Then, he was as Spanish as any of them, and like most Spanish men left the day-to-day manifestations, the recurrent prayers, the activities before the house altar, to the women and the children. At that time, too, he had a mild feud of obscure origin with Father Mueller.

Rociada was one of Father Mueller's many *visitas*. His home church was at Sápello; from there he rode out endlessly on his big raw-boned white horse to one remote settlement after another over a network of appalling roads. The spaces were vast, the life rugged, the contributions meager. It was a parish for such a man as Father Mueller, a strong, big, heavy, black-bearded Austrian, rough, uncouth, and learned. He was no longer young, but he was untiring, and a magnificent eater. When he came to Rociada to hold services at the church of Santo Niño de Atocha, he stayed at the Bacas'. Everyone of any consequence did. His splendid consumption of food at Doña Marguerite's excellent table would not be checked by the accident that, an hour or so earlier, he had stopped off at Seña Dionisia's house — Seña Dionisia being rated as about the best cook of pastry, *enchiladas,* and *sopaipillas* in the neighborhood — and in the course of conversation eaten a whole pie and drunk a pot of coffee.

He was enormously fond of children. His way of playing with them was rough, as was so much of his humor, and he was given to pinching them painfully, but the three little girls enjoyed him. He would play hide-and-seek with them as if he were their own age, all over the house and under the beds, and he tolerated the most outrageous impudences. Once that year Carmen, being then nine, found him asleep in an armchair on the porch, where he was awaiting her mother's return. She slipped his broad-brimmed, black, worn felt hat off his head, put leaves, sticks, and a grasshopper in it, and put it back on. When Doña Marguerite arrived the priest leaped to his feet and, half awake, gave her a sweeping Austrian bow that resulted in a distribution of the contents of his hat immediately at her feet.

His hostess did not have to be told that one of the children had been up to tricks, and she was prepared to be angry, but Father Mueller laughed so delightedly that she gave up. He tolerated many such indignities — once, even, when Consuelo was sitting in his lap and supposedly lighting his cigar, laughing inwardly at her attempts, in a spirit of experimentation, to set fire "accidentally" to his beard. All the Baca children had the Western propensity for practical jokes, and while the three youngest speak even today of how rough Father Mueller was, it is a question in my mind whether they, delicately pretty, ladylike little creatures that they were, were not his match.

His relations with the older three were less cordial. Pino, as I have said, was vaguely at odds with him. Emilie, definitely a young lady, found him uncouth; their relations were formal. Marie, youngest of the older group, had entered her teens and no longer enjoyed his romps, which rather hurt him. He paid her and Pino back in his own fashion, by such means as, when the time came for the collection in church, announcing, "Handsome Pino will pass the plate, and pass it first to proud Marie."

One never knew what he would come out with during a service. He excoriated sinners by name and with full details. Mass was said at Rociada at irregular intervals and the priest had no time for training his altar boys himself, so they never became really proficient; his instructions to them during the service were audible and vigorously worded. He was impressive in his own way, but it would never have occurred to Carmen, Consuelo, or Pepita that he might be God's chosen instrument for the punishment of their brother.

What first got them to thinking that Pino was headed for trouble with the Almighty was an incident when he was home for Christmas during his last year of boarding school. They were already annoyed with his superiorities when the evening came on which Father Mueller rode over to perform a baptism. He arrived near sundown, his big horse weary from plodding through snow, his hat and his big black cape powdered from a flurry he had ridden through. The sun was off the valley, the snow outside the house was turning from blue to various shades of purple, strongest in color close to the contrasting rectangles where the yellow lamplight fell upon it. His arrival caused the usual disturbance as the dogs rushed out, spooking his horse and making it whirl. Canuto, the Negro, went to hold his horse and take his saddlebags, and he swung down with his cloak flapping.

It was late dusk when Father Mueller opened his saddlebags to get something, and then he made outcry. The worn strap which closed the left-hand pocket had broken and the Holy Oils had fallen out. If they could not be found, it would be a tragedy in more than one way. No priest would take lightly the suggestion that he might have been careless with anything as sacred as the Oils; Father Mueller had not been, save insofar as that he used bags as worn and old as the rest of his outfit. Then, the Oils are blessed only once a year, on Holy Thursday, at the cathedral. The priest did not carry his store for the year on his saddle when he made his rounds, but the loss of what he had with him could be serious. If he should run short before the year was out, he would have to make a round trip of some two hundred miles between Sápello and the cathedral city of Santa Fe to obtain more.

Everyone ran out, with lamps and flashlights — everyone except the lordly Pino. He, after he had performed the proper courtesies on the priest's first arrival, had sunk into an armchair by the fire and lost himself in a magazine. There he stayed put.

The horse had swerved out of the cleared area immediately in front of the veranda steps when the dogs ran out at him, so that Father Mueller had dismounted in deep snow. There they found one sock, with holes in toe and heel, and a pack of wheat-straw cigarette paper, lying on the surface, so they were fairly sure that it was there, too, that the Oils had fallen out when Canuto took off the saddlebags. Their small, heavy container, of course, would have sunk deep in the fluffy snow. The Bacas, the priest, and Canuto searched and searched, without result, until the bitter cold of after dark drove them in.

Without the appropriate Oil, there could be no baptism. Don José contemplated his son, comfortable by the fire. He told him that he should get out the Ford and drive to Sápello for more Oil, so that the baptism could be performed as scheduled. He had better start right away, Don José said, so as to get there before the sacristan went to bed. Father Mueller wrote a note to the sacristan and handed it to Pino with hearty expressions of appreciation of his kindness.

It would never have occurred to the boy to protest an order of his father's, but it was plain enough that he was thoroughly unhappy at having to drive some thirty miles of snowy road at night, and just when he could hear and smell supper being put on the table. Carmen, seeing his darkened face as he went out, thought, Serves him right. It was then that she first conceived the idea that her brother might be getting in bad with God.

At bedtime she confided this idea, which in the meantime she had elaborated considerably, to Consuelo. It excited them both. Though at this time they thought him bossy, basically they admired and loved their big brother. They did not really wish him harm, but this thought was of a special order, it was awe-inspiring and full of mystery, and somehow it added to Pino's stature. Also, it made a wonderful secret. Later, they told Pepita. As she was only five, she could grasp the significance of the idea even less than they, but she was properly impressed by it, and she had the infant's unruffled interest in death and violence.

Consuelo did suggest that his having had to drive to Sápello that night had been his punishment, but that thought was so anticlimactic that even she rejected it. For the rest of the Christmas vacation, and when Pino returned from school in the spring, by then a full-fledged sub-freshman and behaving accordingly, they watched and tallied the evidences of his sinfulness and waited for God's wrath to manifest itself. What evidences they found seem to have satisfied them, but they must have been made apparent only by a sort of intensive process of reading between the lines.

The feeling that a great event must be impending on the divine level was strengthened by the news, received in the spring, that in August the Archbishop himself would come to Rociada and hold a confirmation service there. That was an event of the first magnitude. When Doña Marguerite was a girl, the great Archbishop Lamy had visited the place from time to time, staying with her parents, M. and Mme. Pendaries, not uninfluenced by the prospect of a French cuisine, a glass of sound wine, and an evening of conversation in his native tongue — but that had been long ago. Not in years had any of his successors come to that part of the mountains. His Grace, of course, would stay at Don José and Doña Marguerite's.

Talk of the event, and first preparations, such as writing to friends in Santa Fe to learn the Archbishop's preferences in food and drink, got going early. For the three girls, the prospect of it made religiosity more dramatic than ever. God's eye would be on Rociada with special attention; it behooved everyone to have his house set in order, his hearth swept. But their big brother, alas, did not seem to realize that.

Then Pino received an Awful Warning. It was shortly after his return from school, when he was supervising the shearing — rather late in the season — of the last bunch of sheep to be shorn on the home ranch. The work was done by an itinerant crew from Old Mexico, a picturesque outfit which served Don José each year. The men wore big sombreros, bright, dirty shirts, and close-fitting trousers of the *charro* cut. Their boss dressed always in a tuxedo, a shirt without a collar, and a very big gray felt sombrero with remnants of gold stitching on it.

It was a hot, sultry afternoon. Several small thunderstorms were roaming about the mountains; one of them looked as if it might come over the ranch. Emilie, having business in the village, and being not at all afraid of lightning, decided to drive there, and offered to take the little girls with her. She told them that a storm might hit the ranch, but that she was pretty sure they would run into none on the road or in the village. The girls ran to get ready. Getting ready was not simple. As it was only two miles to Rociada, the expedition would not justify asking for a lunch, but one should take a cookie for the road, one had to decide which doll should go on the trip, and, since there would be visiting and one never visited empty-handed, gifts to assemble. By the time they all got into the car and Emilie, to avoid endless discussion, had determined for them where each one should sit, the sky to the east and north was black and the blackness reached clear overhead. The actual lightning and rain seemed to be a mile or more away.

Emilie swung the car around and drove by the shearing shed, where they stopped for a minute or so to watch. Threat of clouds and all, it was worth looking at. The shed was a great corrugated iron roof on posts, the space inside being divided into sections by sheep panels about five feet high. The sheep stood bleating in the various sections until, hairless at last, they were turned loose. The shearing was in plain view at the near side of the shed. The Mexicans were using electric clippers, powered by a generator on their truck, which stood just under the eaves. The colorful crew dragged up the squirming sheep one by one. The shearer was skillful; he made the fleece peel off in long, thick strips, and for all the animals' struggling, did not draw a drop of blood. To one side, Pino, in Stetson hat, blue denim, and boots, stood beside the dark figure of the Mexican boss. The light pouring on the men, the animals, and the roof — rust-red with a couple of brilliant strips where new sheets of iron had been put on — had the pale quality of sunlight under clouds. Behind, the dark clouds themselves replaced the sky.

There was a flash of lightning quite near by. Emilie started the motor. Then another came, its peal sounding at the same instant. It struck the iron roof, tearing a hole in it, flashed to the generator, and flared horrifyingly out of the clippers. The sheep being shorn was killed; the shearer was knocked unconscious, partly disrobed, and had all his hair burned off. But the sisters' attention was riveted to what was happening to Pino. While the four of them, having let out one scream, stared, he made a standing jump over the first panel, then took three more as no Olympic hurdler could have done, and disappeared into the meadow, running in great leaps.

Carmen, Consuelo, and Pepita looked at each other. They were speechless; they could not tell their big sister what they believed had happened. Then they saw Pino coming back. He was pale and shaken, sweat broke out all over him, but he was unharmed, and as he came near, recovering himself, he began swearing intensely. Emilie asked him if he was all right. He said he thought he was. He went back into the shed to inspect the damage. Emilie let out the clutch.

When they were alone, the girls had some discussion as to whether God could have missed His aim. They concluded that that was impossible. It had been an Awful Warning — totally wasted, for look how he had cursed when he should have been on his knees. Sadly, but with appreciation, they contemplated the picture of this handsome, grown-up brother who was bent on destroying himself. And with the Archbishop coming, they agreed, the final punishment would not be long delayed.

Early in the summer, the older children had school friends from the East to visit. With them in the house, Pino was more the man and the lordly elder brother than ever. This led to a series of minor conflicts, which the trio interpreted as further evidence of the sad condition of his soul. Carmen particularly feuded with him; she was not only certain that his doom was at hand, she was heartily in favor of it. It would be more correct to say that Consuelo feared that she was right. Secretly, she prayed that his punishment be mitigated. When she was alone, she inclined to think that having to drive to Sápello that winter *had* been a penance, that she and her sisters were sometimes annoying, and that any man would have cursed after the shock of the lightning. When she was with

Carmen, however, these hopeful doubts faded.

The time of the Archbishop's visit drew near. Father Mueller worked like fury, traveling from settlement to settlement to perfect the candidates for confirmation and instruct the ablest of his altar boys. Every eligible child in the parish was in line to be confirmed, as parents seized the chance to have it done near home instead of having to take their children to Las Vegas. From Sápello on, where there were settlements or even a single farm by the road, the people built arches of green branches and decorated them with flowers and paper streamers, while Rociada village and the Santo Niño de Atocha were buried in adornments. Everyone in the village was cooking like mad, to be ready for the flood of visitors.

Doña Marguerite's house was in a thorough turmoil. The Archbishop would arrive one afternoon, have supper, and then the following day, after the services, would be the guest of honor at what had to be a memorable dinner. For Consuelo, the rising tempo of preparations caused a parallel crescendo of anticipation, and as the activities, not only in her mother's house but in the whole community, were on a scale she had never known before, they impressed her ever more deeply with the importance of the coming event.

On the day the Archbishop was due, from early morning, people were passing along the road in front of the ranch. Consuelo was torn between hanging on the veranda rail to watch them, and going inside to keep track of the household activities, now approaching frenzy. The people came on foot, often carrying infants, some of them dusty after fifteen or twenty miles of travel. Men, boys, a few girls and younger women, came by on horseback; older women seldom rode, and the young ones, slacks being considered no costume for females, sat their horses unselfconsciously with their skirts of necessity barely reaching their knees. Wagons and buggies formed a procession, and occasionally a motor would weave its way past them. The people came from Sápello, Peñasco Blanco, Upper Rociada, and Gascón, from Ledoux, San Ignacio, Cow Creek, and Las Tusas. They came from the solitary little farms in the side canyons that have names only to those who live close by them, from the branches of the creeks, and from the lost, green, snow-enriched valleys.

Don José arrived from Las Vegas, bringing the Archbishop, in the midafternoon, driving him past the house directly to the church for the first formalities. From the village, the children heard the church bells ringing, and the slow, respectful banging of rifles fired in the air. It was late in the day before the party reached the ranch. The Archbishop, a Franciscan, was everything the girls had hoped, impressive in the old-style, gray robe, with his purple biretta and purple at his throat. With him were Father Mueller and his secretary, in the more usual, Franciscan brown.

His Grace said he was due to read his breviary, so Don José cleared everyone off the porch and warned all the household to be quiet. Consuelo slipped out and hid under a lilac bush to watch the tall, robed figure, book in hand, absorbed, walking up and down the porch with his slow, slightly rocking, priestly gait. She thought that he must at this moment be talking with God far more closely and intimately than ever he could in public prayer at church. God must be very near at hand. She made a little prayer for Pino; she did not exactly pray to the Archbishop, but she aimed it so that it might carom off him and receive extra strength.

As far as the Bacas were concerned, without irreverence the climax of the whole occasion was not the Mass the following morning, but the dinner for which the household had been turned upside down. The Mass had been impressive, and the sense of it carried over, so that the meal, which was served shortly after two in the afternoon, was a sort of sanctified celebration, an occasion of good eating and joviality made happier, not stiffer, by its association with an important religious event. It was a big party at the table, an assortment of Baca and Pendaries relatives and the leading people of the district as well as the clerics and the immediate family. They were gay. The Archbishop was pleased with the way things had gone, Father Mueller was relieved and triumphant. The sherry was *oloroso,* the claret excellent, and both wines were the more relished now that prohibition was in force.

Pino, dressed to the nines with a formal, stiff collar and his hair well slicked down, chanced to be seated next to Father Mueller. Under the influence of the occasion, they had forgotten the coolness between them. They were talking together when the priest's attention was caught by Pino's handkerchief, projecting in neat folds above his pocket. Looked at more closely, it seemed to be unlike any handkerchief the priest had ever seen, at least in the possession of a man. Father Mueller was on his best behavior, but curiosity and a faint suspicion as to the nature of the object caused him to revert to his ordinary self. With the unexpected quickness of a bear in action, he reached out and pulled forth the handkerchief.

When he saw what he had, he roared and held it high. The table became a tempest of laughter. The handkerchief was a novelty bought a short time before in Las Vegas, the last word in trimmings for the dashing young blade — a miniature pair of pink lace-trimmed panties. Doña Marguerite seemed to choke. Don José flushed, then broke out laughing. The two older girls were torn; they were furious at their brother for disgracing the family, yet they could not keep straight faces. Over the general uproar, Canuto's unrestrained delight made a sort of obligato. Aside from Doña Marguerite, only the three little girls were relatively quiet. They looked at the panties, at their brother's face, then at each other, and dissolved into weak uncontrollable giggles. It was so perfect, it was so just exactly what he had coming to him. Consuelo's delight was reinforced by profound relief; this was the punishment, and it would not destroy her brother. They kept on giggling thereafter, softly, one at a time or when one caught another's eye, until Pino could have murdered them.

Father Mueller handed back the object and Pino crammed it into a side pocket. He stared at his plate, toyed with his food, wished he could die. He could hear Emilie, Marie, and some of his cousins on the subject for months to come. Conversation resumed again, but almost five minutes later, when no one was speaking, the Archbishop gave a sudden, short laugh. One could not leave the table until the long meal had reached its end and the Archbishop had given thanks. No one hurried. It was an interminable penance.

The priestly party left in time to reach Las Vegas by dusk. The house, the air, seemed empty. Consuelo swung on the gate. God had acted, and with mercy — perhaps in answer to her prayers. But there was a new, big thing to wonder over — no one had ever suggested to her that God might punish with laughter.

V

The Snow Too Deep

WHEN CONSUELO was a little girl Christmas loomed up brilliant long in advance. What she had been told by her older brother and older sisters — especially Carmen, just two years her senior and still free of disillusionment — what she herself remembered, and what she invented in telling her little sister, Pepita, about the delightful sights and experiences of the feast of Christmas all combined as simple fact. The short reach of her memory seemed long, as long as the meaning of "always." It had always happened like this; it always would. And the pleasure of anticipation grew stronger each year. One began thinking of Christmas with the first frosts, along about the time one began thinking of snow and sleds. Another Christmas was on its way, as certain as the seasons themselves. If anyone had suggested that the seasons were uncertain or that Christmas itself might fail, probably she would not have understood, and if she had, more than likely she would have rejected the thought as foolish, or the kind of tasteless humor some grownups indulge in.

How it happened that the Bacas developed the magnificent Christmas celebration they did puzzles me. Don José came of a family of purely Spanish descent that was powerful in the region about Las Vegas, New Mexico, on the southern slopes of the Sangre de Cristo Mountains. He must have been reared in a strongly Spanish tradition, and he had something of his ancestors' cultural orientation toward Spain, through Mexico City as the point of linkage and distribution — much as many educated Western Anglo-Americans retain an orientation toward Britain through New York. He procured his bride's wedding chest from the southern capital and took her there on her honeymoon, and it was there, too, that he later found a governess for his younger daughters. As I have told, although Doña Marguerite grew up at Rociada, she was reared in a strongly French tradition.

One would expect, then, that Don José and Doña Marguerite would delight their children with the songs and processions of the *posadas,* the breaking of *piñatas* — fanciful pottery birds filled with small gifts — or the setting of shoes by the fireplace to receive *étrennes* on New Year's Eve. Actually, apart from Mass on Christmas Day, with its singing of the ancient *alabados* — hymns of praise — the only exotic touch to their celebration was serving tamales in the course of the morning, a pleasant custom to which all New Mexico, Anglo- or Spanish-American, subscribes. For the rest, they observed the Anglo-Dutch practices centering around Santa Claus and the tree — but without the business of stockings — in a manner to make almost anyone retrospectively envious.

The day before Christmas there would be no sign of tree or gifts; if you did not know for sure, you might wonder if there would be any. The preparations for the huge dinner on Christmas afternoon, however, began days in advance and could not be concealed. Doña Marguerite is a petite, brisk woman with a neat, fast step; the recurrent clicking of her heels when she is at work on a feast is unmistakable. Even in a big house, one would catch the sound, along with her instructions — in Spanish to the maids, in English with occasional spurts of French to her two older daughters — her exclamations of despair over the whole project when something went wrong, occasionally her annoyance, and her helpers answering her in kind and with equal feeling. During these preparations Carmen, Consuelo, and Pepita were in the kitchen as much as they were allowed to be, dainty, black-haired, oval-faced, large-eyed, voracious little creatures savoring a delicious torment.

The indications of great eating to come were titillating in themselves but even more exciting because they were the sign of the greater wonder that would precede the feast. Christmas Eve was quiet; the little girls were full of expectation and on their best behavior. They had supper early, as always, and afterward they passed the evening until bedtime as nearly as possible as on other evenings. At the usual hour they were sent to bed, but on this one night the three of them slept together in a big fourposter, and, moreover, on this night alone Count, the bloodhound, was allowed in the room with them and took his place at the foot of the bed. They thought they would not be able to sleep; they hoped to stay awake. For a time they whispered, but in the end sleep always captured them.

In the dead of night, as it seemed to them — somewhere between ten and eleven o'clock — they were wakened by the loud ringing of sleigh bells, not at a distance on the road but close at hand and overhead. They knew, of course, that the sound came from on top of the roof. They were into slippers and dressing gowns by the time their mother came for them, but just as the traitor drowsiness always overcame them, so they were never quick enough to get downstairs in time to catch a glimpse of Santa Claus.

Behind him, he left the miracle of the Christmas tree, fully expected and yet breath-stopping, so that you had to stand for a moment in the doorway and absorb it before you went in. It was always a fragrant, fresh-cut fir, tall enough almost to touch the ceiling of that high-ceilinged room, decorated, candle-lit, with the presents massed at its foot. And part of the special quality of the occasion came from the fact that it all took place so late at night after that glorious awakening. Soon after Santa Claus had passed by, visitors from the village would begin to drop in for a glass of wine and a bit of fruitcake. These arrivals, usually one man at a time, occasionally a man and wife, out of the snow and cold — the slight stamping inside the door and the removal of outer garments, the gesture of brushing rime off a heavy mustache, the people formal, rustic, and yet socially graceful, Don José's and Doña Marguerite's welcoming Spanish, the faint smell of wine to spice the smells of the tree, the candles, and the fire — were an essential part of Consuelo's impression of the real beginning of Christmas.

That was the way it was, with the day of prayer and fine eating to come after. That was how it had always been and always would be — until the year of the big snow. In the autumn of that year, an exceptionally early snowfall, in the latter part of September, turned the three little girls' thoughts toward Christmas. The snow was gone within twenty-four hours, but then it was unseasonably cold, not only at night but also in the daytime, which was most unusual before December. Don José studied weather reports and the almanacs, talked to Las Vegas on the hand-cranked telephone, and consulted with Señor Juan. When it snowed again before the month was out, and the white covering, thin though it was, lay for over a week in the shade and was slow to melt even on the sunny slopes, he sent a number of teams to the city to bring back a supply of cottonseed cakes.

The Bacas' Wineglass-2 ranch operation was conducted in good part on the land that Doña Marguerite's father had originally owned, grazed under National Forest permits, or leased. It lay within the mountains, which meant that Don José wintered several thousand head of his sheep, his beef herd, and most of his horses on what was properly summer range. The animals were held within fairly easy reach of Rociada, on pastures where trees and cliffs gave shelter and south slopes caught the sun's full strength, and they were carried through that part of the winter during which they could not rustle for themselves by the rich store of hay harvested from the Rociada meadows. As far back as anyone could remember, that had sufficed, but this year the signs were not good.

It started snowing in earnest the second week of October. Sleds and sleighs appeared early. In that favored land it is unusual for snow to last more than a week or so anywhere that the sun strikes, until one passes above the eight-thousand-foot level, but this year the cold held through the brightest days even in the valleys. The nights were bitter. What at first had seemed to the children an early, extra bonus of winter fun became too much of a good thing.

November carried on from where October left off. Several times Amadeo Lobato was a day late with the mail, having been unable to get through with his buggy. Automobiles were little used; they remained in their shelters, their radiators drained. Week by week, the snow grew deeper. Don José was constantly out on horseback, plowing his way to this camp or that, or to the horse pasture, to make sure that the men did not relax their efforts under the conditions they faced. Getting the feed to the various pastures was a constant battle of seizing upon the spells of clear weather to break open the roads — no more than cross-country cart tracks, at best — and then stockpiling as rapidly as possible.

Along in December, Don José began feeding the cottonseed cakes to the animals, to supplement the hay, which otherwise would not last through the long feeding period he foresaw. The animals were not ranging at all; they bunched together in narrow trampled areas where the shelter was best. The mail came through erratically. Other traffic with Las Vegas and the railroad was almost completely stopped. A few men from Rociada village, who still believed that the game laws were nothing but an unwarranted attempt to restrict their traditional rights, and who were hardy enough to fight their way through the drifts, built up their family stocks with snowbound deer and elk.

Consuelo heard her father say that the herders were feeding cakes to the sheep; the idea pleased her. It was nice for the poor sheep out in the frozen distances to be given a little cake. One day when she had made her way to the barn, she examined the stuff. It looked like cake. She asked Juan Grande, who was there, and he said yes, those were *queques*. She took one, turned it over in her hands, examined it. It looked like spicecake and had a promising heaviness. She tried it. It was foul, oily, revolting; she could not spit the stuff out fast enough. It was days before she forgave Juan for laughing at her.

In all other years, on a bright day in mid-December the younger children and Doña Marguerite would take a wagon, or go on foot, driving a burro, to gather what they miscall kinnikinnick. This is a ground vine, known as *toje* in the local Spanish. It has close-massed, shiny dark green leaves and red berries, and makes an excellent substitute for holly. Properly speaking, kinnikinnick is a mixture of the dried leaves and bark of certain plants, used by the Indians (the word is of Algonquian origin) as a substitute for tobacco, or to mix with it. As far as I know, no one smokes the ground vine. The trips for kinnikinnick were picnics, the last of the year — gay occasions, bright with small adventures, charged with the imminence of Christmas. They were the first preparation for the great event. There was no question of any such expedition this year, which was not going like any other. The unchangeable had been changed.

When Doña Marguerite recalls the winter of the big snow, she is likely to speak of what happened to Mr. Goldfarb — "such a nice man, poor thing." Goldfarb's story, in its main outlines, was a classic one of the western frontier — the merchant who came out to the new country with a stock-in-trade he could carry on his back or pack on a single mule and, by intense thrift and drive, built that stake up into a solid business. It differed in that this man came West comparatively late; nonetheless, after twenty industrious years he was within reaching distance of at least modest wealth.

That fall, the prices of sheep and wool were at a record low, as a result of the slump following the First World War, but there were signs that times were improving and that sheep and wool, like other commodities, were due to rise sharply before spring. Goldfarb saw his opportunity. Putting up his store in Las Vegas as security, he raised all the money his credit would stand and invested it in a flock of slightly over three thousand ewes and the corresponding complement of rams, the latter mostly registered stock. To winter them, he leased several miles of good grass on an open, level, almost treeless mesa top south of Las Vegas. Ideally, he should have leased lower country, but in ordinary years sheep wintered well on that range.

The region of Las Vegas is notoriously a place of driving winter winds. That year, the snow-laden winds prowled like a siege of wolves. The coyotes came out of the mountains early, to skulk about the edges of the city and awaken the dogs to frenzy, until the nights were maniacal with barking and the answering, challenging, mocking howls. Out on the open mesas, the snow drove and piled, and there, too, the predators quested.

Goldfarb's herders were simply hired hands. There were no old friendships and family loyalties between him and them to induce them to maintain punishing vigilance despite the whip of the winter. He himself, with his business to run, could not be constantly visiting the camps. Snow, sleet, wind, and cold made the men keep close to their huts and their fires. The sheep drifted, looking for shelter that did not exist, until they fetched up against the fences. By December the covering of ice and snow was too deep for them to scrape through it to grass, and they could not fight through its cold mass to find and browse on those bushes and shrubs that still reached the surface. The snow piled on the animals as they huddled. When God sent a bright, still noon, the snow melted; at sundown it froze into little cloud-colored balls of ice on their wool.

The sheep had to be fed. Goldfarb went to buy hay, as many others were doing. The going price that fall had been fifteen dollars a ton, baled and delivered; suddenly it was sixty dollars and haul it yourself, and he had no more credit. As his sheep hungered and grew weak, the coyotes moved in on them, but the wild beasts could not kill as fast as cold and starvation. Before the month was out, there was nothing left of his twenty years of effort but the frozen carcasses on the mesa.

If the snow was white and cold and deep below Las Vegas, in the mountain valleys it was just as gleamingly white, and colder and deeper. Day after day, Don José and Señor Juan put on their sheepskin-lined jackets, pulled their chaps over their heaviest trousers, muffled the lower part of their faces, and rode out to the camps, to return weary, cold, hungry, with icicles on the mufflers across their mouths. Day after day, the men went up on the roof of the big ranchhouse to shovel off snow, and sometimes in the night Consuelo wakened to the sound of the shovels scraping overhead. There was no longer such a thing as a mail day; Amadeo was using a sleigh with a team, and even so he rarely got through to the ranch.

When their parents suggested to the girls that Santa Claus might not be able to make it that year, they did not at first believe it possible that this could happen. It took time for them to accustom themselves to the idea that there could be winters too severe for even a saint who lived at the North Pole to travel through, and to accept the uncertainty of what they had supposed the most certain thing in life. It was an acceptance that did not come easily.

The paths between the big house and the bunkhouse, the commissary, and the barns had become trenches with walls nearly as high as a man's head. The children played in them, exploring a novelty. These, they decided, were what was meant by the word "tunnel." When the sun was out, it made a bright zone along the upper part of one wall; it edged the opposite crest with jewels. Below, the shade was luminous. On a day of overcast, Consuelo, on some errand of her own, stopped midway in a tunnel. With her mittened hand, she scraped at one wall. She decided to make a *nicho,* in which she might set a saint modeled of snow. She scraped away until, her hand getting chilled through the red wool, she stopped to warm it under her armpit. This was the snow that was too deep for Santa Claus. She looked up, considering its depth. Above, the sky was leaden; it made her feel the dead weight of winter and the promise of yet more flakes shortly. It was not the thickness of the cold white blanket that would stop Santa, she decided; it was the whole nature of the season. Without having words for it, she felt the smothering quality of *too much.* The tunnel became desolate. She would not put a saint there, a snow saint, a cold saint. She hurried back to the house.

Ordinarily, the three girls liked to lie in front of the fire evenings and watch the gold sparks that winked and ran through the soot at the back. They called the sparks Indians, and made a game of counting them. Now, without anything being said, they dropped this game. Everything to do with the fireplace was a reminder of Christmas, and the erratic, ascending course of the spark Indians had too often carried their thoughts on, up, and out to the North Pole.

Pino came home from college. He reached Rociada, thanks to a favorable break in the weather. Don José was able to reach Sápello in the sleigh, and Pino got that far from Las Vegas in a car driven by a cousin. Hardly was he in the house before he had on his boots, his chaps, and the rest of his gear to take over some of the burden of patroling the camps. It was time, too, to throw the rams in with the ewes, and under the circumstances the big creatures had to be carted to the flocks.

So far, the stock was wintering well; their shelter was good, and there was adequate feed for them. The principal trouble was with the coyotes raiding the sheep. The coyotes had grown bold, and in the freezing nights the dogs were not always able to keep them off. To the eastward there was a special breed of beasts of prey, descendants of coyotes and a variety of hound that a rancher had imported to hunt them but that had fraternized instead. Pino once described them as the "most marauderous animals" he had ever known.

Don José and Pino decided that Pino could probably get through to Las Vegas by car, so three days before Christmas he set out on a last-minute sortie for green vegetables, celery, fruit, and Christmas gifts for the youngsters. He did get to the city and accomplish his shopping, but on the way back, late in the day, his motor failed on Nine Mile Hill, some forty miles from home, and he had to stay there until a man in a wagon gave him a lift back to Las Vegas, well after sundown. One of his ears was frozen. He got home by relays, on Christmas Eve, virtually empty-handed, with his ear swollen and black. Amadeo had managed another mail delivery that morning.

Carmen, Consuelo, and Pepita by then were in full

mourning over the defeat of Santa Claus. They cheered up somewhat when their parents told them that the whole family would have supper together and at the grownups' hour. They would eat in the kitchen, Doña Marguerite said, instead of in the dining room, to save fuel. They all sat down — Don José, Doña Marguerite, Pino, and the three little girls. The two older girls, one at college, one at boarding school, had not come home for this holiday. Christmas Eve being a day of fast, the meal was meatless and simple, but good — *chicos, tortitas de huevos, chile colorado* made without meat, and other such fast-day dishes, which are delicacies in themselves. The parents led the conversation around to the variety of Christmas customs among different peoples, and especially to the custom of hanging stockings to be filled by Santa Claus. The girls were interested; the subject, although painful, was fascinating. They discussed the pros and cons of Christmas stockings, and considered the very odd idea, proffered by their mother, that one might have these but no Christmas tree.

When the meal had ended, the family still remained at the table, talking. Suddenly Don José stiffened, listening. Everyone fell silent. "What was that I heard?" he said.

Carmen said immediately, "Sleigh bells!"

They all listened intently. Definitely there was a sound of bells, but was it outside or in the living room? The three girls were out of their chairs instantly. Carmen managed to whisper "Santa" in a way that had the quality of a shout; then they were on the run, through the dining room to the living room, their elders following more sedately. Consuelo was in the lead, because her chair had been nearest the door.

As they broke into the living room, they slowed down, not knowing quite what to expect. There was no tree, but the mantelpiece was rich with boughs and ornaments, and under these hung three of their stockings — the sturdy, long, woollen ones — bulging with gifts. The three little girls went to them almost timidly.

Naturally, they did not notice that all their presents were of the kind usually purchased from the mail-order houses; even had they known enough for that, they would never have thought to scrutinize a miracle. Santa Claus had made it, after all — with a light pack, to be sure, for obvious reasons, but he had made it. When their parents and Pino had had time to express their astonishment, they handed the stockings down to the children. The two maids and Juan Chico, who had not been in the kitchen during supper, came in from the hall and added their exclamations. The children settled down before the fire, blissful with their presents. It was already past their bedtime, but Doña Marguerite said nothing. Shortly, Amadeo and Tomás Lobato knocked at the door, stamping and brushing off snow, and Doña Marguerite sent one of the maids for the fruitcake while Don José brought the decanter of sherry from the dining room. Everything was in order, and Christmas was a certainty after all.

Consuelo went to bed hugging a new fluffy rabbit. Tucked in, she lay feeling the cold that seeped in through the narrow opening at the bottom of the window. She heard the faint thud and squeak of horses plodding in over cold snow, the icy jingle of a spur, and a man's voice speaking wearily. That would be Señor Juan and one of the hands coming in late from a mission to one of the farther camps. She was glad that they would soon be in the warmth. She snuggled farther down in the bed with the rabbit, mentally telling it her secret, a secret more wonderful even than Christmas stockings or gifts. She had been first into the living room, and she had seen — with her own eyes she, and she only, had seen — Santa Claus's red-clad legs and his boots just disappearing up the chimney.

VI

The News from Rociada

ONE OF THE MOST surprising of all the elements in Canuto's relationship with the Bacas is that, remarkable and strange though they found him on first acquaintance, and strange though such a family must have been to an Alabama Negro, neither he nor they saw anything surprising in his incorporation into their household. To me, when I first joined the family, he was flatly astonishing.

Canuto came to Rociada along about 1922, when Consuelo was still tending her dolls. Her brother and her two older sisters, having been away to school and to college, had seen something of Negroes but had never properly known any. In New Mexico in the twenties men of that race were a rarity; the three youngest children had occasionally glimpsed a Negro — and that was all — in Las Vegas.

Doña Marguerite first heard of Canuto's presence in the neighborhood of Rociada from women of the village. They said that a young man, *un vaquero negro, un moro,* who tended a small bunch of cattle in the rough country to the westward, was coming into the valley to peddle milk from the cows. Doña Marguerite said, "*Válgame!*" and laughed in astonishment. The news astonished and diverted everyone. The presence of a Moor was remarkable; the idea of extracting from range cows even a few quarts of milk, to be carried down on horseback to sell, all but stopped the imagination.

How Canuto got to New Mexico is unclear; how he received his Spanish name no one knows. All the years before he came to the Rociada country seem to have belonged to another, distinct incarnation, of which he remembers not his own experiences but tidings of someone else's adventures. When he came, he had a vague impression of his native Alabama, a memory of his mother, and certain songs, which never left him.

It is clear that somewhere between his tenth and twelfth years, perhaps in 1905, with white people he crossed the Mississippi on the train at Baton Rouge. Why he was traveling, who those people were who took him remain unknown. In some sequence, also now lost, he was in Chicago, in Wisconsin, in Tennessee. There must have been "points between," but we have no news of them. We do know that, having become a young man — broad-shouldered, of medium height, very strong, very dark — after much traveling and much changing of employers, he reached New Mexico.

By then, he had some knowledge of the arts of the cowboy, of cookery, and of service within the house. He could read slowly and, with slow effort, write a little. A family named Caulfield brought him into the mountains, to tend a little bunch of cattle they were running from a leased ranch on the road to Peñasco Blanco, a few miles from the Bacas' home ranch.

The Caulfields were Southerners, with pretensions of aristocracy and a reality of poverty. They picked Canuto up in Las Vegas, which is the metropolis and the gateway of the high northeastern country. Las Vegas lies at an altitude of sixty-four hundred feet, but the Rociada people think of it as being in the lowlands, outside the massif of the Sangre de Cristo Mountains. From there, with the Caulfields, Canuto turned north and westward on the dirt road that winds always deeper into the real mountains until it runs in the valley of a muddy stream, which near Sápello becomes a clear little river, and so upward, following wide, canyon-walled valleys threaded by successive watercourses, into the country of the big pines, the aspens, and the brilliant meadows, to the wide, hill-guarded valley of Rociada.

News of Canuto's presence there spread fast. At first he was nameless, a strange figure, a phenomenon. Those who had spoken with him said that he knew almost no Spanish and distorted what he did know strangely, while his English they, with their little English, found incomprehensible. Then, without explanation, he became Canuto, the single name, like a character in an old tale. The extreme poverty that was expressed in his ragged clothing and his desperate dairy enterprise formed part of his legend — and led to the notation that the Caulfields (that unpronounceable name!) were in no sense *patrones*. When a poor man hired another, both lived in equal poverty and upon the same social plane; there was no question of a *patrón.* When people of any degree of social pretension maintained even one hired hand, it was expected that they would consider his welfare as a part of their own.

Canuto's presence was a great thing; here was someone to talk about, and even the smallest item of new information about the Negro was eagerly received, a subject to remain fresh for a long time. Sápello, the Pecos valley, Mora, the ranches of the Cimarrón country — none of them had ever possessed *un moro.*

From time to time, Canuto drove the Caulfields' wagon to the Baca ranch to buy bran at Don José's mill. While there, he might make a small purchase — coffee, a sack of the cheapest tobacco, some flour — at the commissary. Don José liked his looks and his good manners; himself a *patrón* whose whole enterprise depended upon a network of mutual loyalties, between employer and employed, between ranch and villages, he appreciated Canuto's loyalty to his employers. He told the young man to come to him if he should ever find himself out of work.

The children saw him first on these visits, a ragged figure in the faded blue of his calling, standing in the wagon, swaying slightly, gracefully, to its jolting, handling his team neatly. The rich deep color of his face and hands and the rounded, softened contours of his features enchanted them. Standing in a row, holding hands, the three little girls would watch him go by. They knew better, but they could not help thinking that perhaps he was masked, like the clown in the Matachine Dance the villagers sometimes performed on the fiesta of Santo Niño de Atocha.

Canuto was trying to feed himself by selling milk — an impossibility, considering the amount it is possible to get from a dozen or so range cows by roping and tying them, and agilely stealing a little of their fluid while standing off their hungry calves. The Caulfields gave Canuto virtually nothing; their poor little cattle venture existed at all only because their servant, for whatever reason, was willing to sacrifice himself to it. Dire need drove Canuto to other shifts. In the course of his wanderings, he had learned a special technique of stealing turkeys. His method was to scatter powdered sulphur in their pen; this the birds would peck eagerly, then shortly they would fall asleep. After that, it was a matter only of selecting the ones to put in his sack; there was no noise to call out the owner.

Over toward Sápello, an Anglo-American named Sibley was raising turkeys. Canuto went to Sibley's place, with a success that baffled the owner. For Sibley to maintain a watch outside until the thief returned was impracticable; only after a long wait would Canuto again levy tribute. The turkey-stealing went on thus for some months, until one night Canuto's supply of sulphur was too small. A turkey woke and squawked, Sibley came out with a rifle, and Canuto was in trouble.

The Caulfields promptly abandoned their man. Sibley, angry over the loss of his turkeys, wanted blood. Don José suggested to him that he should go easy, but Sibley would have none of it. Friendless, Canuto came up for trial and was sentenced to two years in the state penitentiary.

Not many months after that Don José became lieutenant-governor of New Mexico. When Canuto had served his minimum term, Don José arranged for the young man to be paroled to him. By then, Canuto was a trusty, serving as the warden's cook. Don José brought him back to Rociada and gave him a place in the household.

To the people of that section, the fact that a man had done time had none of the automatic significance it would have in, for instance, my own native village in New England. They considered not the isolated fact of the sentence but the nature of the man and of the offense. Offhand I can name four from thereabouts who have been in the pen. To only one, a Mexican who settled there and turned out to be truly criminal, does opprobrium attach; for the others, the feeling is best expressed in the literal meaning of our expression "He fell foul of the law."

The law is rigid; it was devised by strangers for controlling other strangers, for faceless people without names. When it reaches into the quiet stream of life in the mountains, like a bear pawing for trout, and flips one of one's own out onto the bank, one can only be philosophical about it. Everyone knows that Fulano, say, is a good workman, a good neighbor; everyone knows what led him to the action for which he is being punished. Everyone is glad when a good man comes home, free to return to a useful life.

Canuto came to the ranch under no cloud. The cloud, rather, fell upon the Caulfields, who had vanished. They were blamed for having kept him in such poverty and for having deserted him when he was in trouble. To a lesser degree, the cloud cast its shadow on Sibley. Now that Canuto was part of the rambling nexus in which it was difficult to say where household ended and community began, he was included in the wide range of the Bacas' loyalty. They were angry at his former employers, and even after twenty-five years they still feel some resentment toward Sibley for his prosecution.

Canuto's arrival at the ranchhouse was dramatic. He rode up from Las Vegas in Pascual Orozco's wagon. Pascual let him out in front of the big house. When he stepped onto the long porch, the dogs went wild, threatening a mass attack. The principal dog, Count, a bloodhound, fastened upon the seat of his trousers and ripped off a big piece. Pino and Doña Marguerite ran out of the house, and Juan Grande, who was in the yard digging in a flowerbed, ran up to the porch, all of them shouting. Consuelo and Pepita had been sitting under their mother's big sewing machine, swinging on the wide treadle. They came out to watch the rumpus. The dogs were called off. Pino threatened to punish them direly; Juan kicked at them without touching them; Doña Marguerite told them plainly what she thought of their behavior and then turned to give the embarrassed newcomer a gracious welcome.

The children followed the grownups into the house and, retiring to their lair under the sewing machine, studied the new personage from safety. They noticed his lively, alert, small eyes and his very large smile; they listened to his strange manner of speech, full of words they had never heard before. Their general impression was that he was indeed something new and quite wonderful.

Don José thought of him as another hand, but Canuto had his own pattern of service, which he insisted on. Indoor work, to the Bacas, was for women, but Canuto worked both indoors and out. He could muck out a stable, drive a team, move a bunch of cattle, tend pigs and chickens, cook, wash dishes, and wait on table. In a white jacket, he served with real elegance. Later in the evening, he could sometimes be induced to sing songs that were to them utterly exotic. He was a past-master of piecrust, pancakes, hot biscuits, and all ways of cooking pork. To these, shortly, under Doña Marguerite's instruction, he added *frijoles con chile, enchiladas,* and *pozole.* There is an element of hearty richness in the native New Mexico cuisine; the French cuisine of Doña Marguerite is something else. Canuto never prospered with those dishes that start with a *roux* or a *bouquet garni,* and demand a delicate exactitude with herbs and butter and more judiciousness than *élan* when it comes to the garlic. He thought he knew how to clean house — the mild, dark-corner-skipping, gracious cleaning of the South. Doña Marguerite introduced him to the detailed, exact, unsparing cleaning of her French inheritance, and under her eye he mastered the practice of it.

Pino found a magnificent use for Canuto. It was his custom to drive to Las Vegas every Saturday for the dances there, taking with him any friend he might have visiting the ranch at the time. To a good Westerner, two hours' driving over bad roads, and the same again when the dance was over, offered no obstacle. The dances were gay, Pino was popular, and Las Vegas was full of warm friends. At midnight it always seemed a shame to stop, so he would invite a few carloads of young people out to Rociada. Then he would telephone the ranch, get Canuto out of bed, and tell him to prepare for eight, ten, or twelve guests.

Canuto would kill as many chickens as he thought needful, make mashed potatoes, cream gravy, and strong coffee, and have the chickens fried and everything ready by the time the party arrived. As a regular thing, the men (as they firmly considered themselves) tipped him generously, a gesture he appreciated as a gesture. From the point of view of monetary return, it was superflous, since the party almost always ended in a crap game in which he cleaned up. Near dawn, the guests might drive back to Las Vegas, or they might stay, the girls sleeping in spare beds and on couches, the men in the haylofts. Waking up to a houseful of guests was neither new nor surprising to Pino's parents; they regarded hospitality as one of the proper uses of a house.

Pino was also at that time a passionate horseman. When he was home, he made the breaking of the ranch's horses his business. Canuto joined him eagerly; he rode well, and had a conviction that he must conquer any horse he tackled. A cinnamon-colored mare Pino sold him threw him twenty-two times, by count, before he mastered her, but not for anything would he have given her up.

Bringing in and riding the wilder of the range horses

was a regular Sunday afternoon diversion, especially when Pino and his two older sisters had guests. Pino rode his share and usually stayed on. Canuto rode his. He fell more often, but whenever he did, he would be bound to ride that horse again, that day or the following Sunday. When he was thrown (and it was always a real twister that threw him), he generally, to the admiration of the onlookers, landed on his head and took no harm from it at all.

To the little girls, it was another part of the wonder of him, watching to see if Canuto would go off on his head. Carmen was then nearly nine. She, Consuelo, and Pepita followed Canuto about the house and grounds. They did everything they could to keep him talking; he was a willing talker, and infinitely patient with them. They could listen to his pronunciation, his voice, his expressions by the hour, and they felt great pride in having a Negro among them.

His charm for them had more to it than that. They could talk with him with an equality they experienced with no other grownup, and enjoy a real meeting of minds. Friendliness and curiosity developed into familiarity, which in the course of time became an outrageous interchange of impudences that continued past childhood. Canuto outdid the girls in backchat and almost always had the last word. To an outsider hearing it for the first time, it was startling. But even an outsider couldn't fail to catch the undertones of relish, and recognize that this was a ritual of affection.

In the three villages Canuto established himself firmly.

He invented a special, private dialect of Spanish, which might have puzzled a formal student of the language but seems always to have been clear to the countryfolk, wherever he went.

The natives liked him, and they found him profoundly comic — not in the sense that they laughed at him, although he didn't mind humor at his own expense, but that they laughed with him. He seemed to be able to show them ways for release in laughter that they could not have found for themselves. He had a personal warmth and an obvious delight in life that warmed the mountain people, who, for all their Latin heritage, were somewhat dour and inturned. Men and women accepted him, respected him, enjoyed him; many of the younger women found him attractive.

Rociada became his home, the Spanish-speaking people of the high country became his people. During most of the year, he worked steadily about the ranch, but at intervals, with months of wages saved up, the craving to wander came over him. He would take a vacation then and set out, an utterly free man, to roam his adopted world. Most often, he proceeded to Las Vegas and from there went on to Santa Fe, the capital, where he was sure of a meal and a fifty-cent piece from the warden of the penitentiary. He visited in the city and tried its fleshpots, and then he went on, northward up the Rio Grande (he gravitated naturally toward the high country and the purely Spanish-American settlements), to the villages on the way to Taos or to the Apache country. Everywhere he found friends, everywhere he had the assurance of a bed and a meal. He was an unfailing novelty, a stimulus; spendthrift, openhanded, loving the Cyrano-like gesture of lavish generosity and also the simple act of giving, he was equally eager to receive.

He always overstayed his leave grossly. By the time he was ready to come back, the Bacas would be waiting for him with anything from a severe tongue-lashing to a discharge, but when he finally turned up — his good clothes dusty and slept-in, he himself broke, footsore, with a dozen lemons or a print of "The End of the Trail" for Doña Marguerite, peanuts or cigars for Pino, red silk stockings, perhaps, for the older girls, a jumble of such gifts in a burlap sack on his back — his appearance, the manner of his entrance, the nature of the things he brought, frustrated anger. The Bacas scolded him roundly, but he was used to that. They were no Anglo-Saxon family; they scolded each other and him, too, in the natural course of events. That was like the sound of rain on the shingled roof of the big house — you stayed in, and you listened to it just enough to know when it stopped, as, in time, it must.

Suddenly, and shockingly, Don José died. About that time, the market for wool and lambs, along with other markets throughout the nation, went to pieces. Not all Doña Marguerite's and Pino's efforts or all the loyalty of their people could keep back a tide that rose like the salt and killing sea. After several years of struggle, the ranch was sold, the Bacas moved to Santa Fe. Canuto went with them.

With the children successively growing up and leaving

their mother's house, there was less and less work for Canuto to do. The room Doña Marguerite had given him remained his *pied-à-terre* and base of operations; he worked in the garden, cleaned house, and turned up to help in the kitchen and wait on table for major functions. The rest of the time, he sought occupation throughout Santa Fe, preferring night work, finding interest and freedom in the dark and lonely city. He was in demand as an occasional butler; there were times when it seemed to Doña Marguerite that she was running an agency, with this hostess and that calling up to reserve Canuto's time. She could not stop with accepting the engagements; she felt it necessary to follow up by making sure that he had a clean white jacket, and, when possible, she liked to look him over before he went to work.

Between his buttling and his night wandering, he acquired stores of gossip, and before long was serving as a sort of local Associated Press; everyone contributed news to him, in exchange for what he broadcast. The sum of all this he would eventually retail to Doña Marguerite while he worked in the house or in the garden. He did not sit and gossip, but neither did he care to work in silence; his periods of activity at home were always of a social nature.

There was an element of magic in his night wanderings. I have never known anyone who so commonly found five- and even ten-dollar bills in the streets. People in a hurry offered him things for sale, from worthless "diamond" rings to valuable luggage — offers he could never refuse. One night, he was standing in a back alley outside a warehouse when an excellent double-barreled shotgun whizzed past his head and landed in the dirt. No claimant for it was ever found; it became Canuto's by default and in time was traded for God alone knows what. He would trade almost anything he had, just for the love of bargaining.

He ate free all over town, he had his room free, and, affecting a raffish raggedness, he very seldom bought new clothes. He was making good money, and he seemed to be able to get rid of it as fast as he made it, between his less successful purchases, his fondness for gambling, and his acts of generosity.

The Bacas felt called upon to get after him for his lack of thrift, as they did for not getting enough sleep, or for sleeping too much, or for not sweeping under the couch, or for setting his breeches on fire by stuffing his hot pipe into a pocket already full of matches. None of this had any effect; he was used to their scolding and he understood its real meaning.

Unknown to them, he did save a considerable sum. Then, one day in 1947, he astounded the family by announcing that he had gone to Rociada and bought an acre of land, on which stood Agapito Gutiérrez's old house. He went ahead and furnished the house, repaired the roof, fenced the land, and set out trees.

From time to time, separately and en masse, according to who might be home at the time, Doña Marguerite, Carmen, Consuelo, and Pepita pointed out to him that he was engaged in utter folly. His irregular weekend trips to his "ranch," more than a hundred miles away, cost him more than it would rent for. Leaving the place unguarded most of the time, he would certainly be robbed blind. He had made a deal with Luis Reyes to water his trees; Luis would probably neglect them. If he put pigs in with Epimenio's on shares, didn't he know that he'd just be feeding Epimenio's pigs for him?

Canuto submitted to all this (one could not say that he listened), as he did to the rest. In season, he brought gifts of venison and trout from Rociada, with details of who had caught the fish or killed the deer, where, and in what manner. In due course, sweetly, without fanfare, he brought fresh young pork for Doña Marguerite's house and for Consuelo's and mine. He supplied us with fresh-churned butter at a price well below the market; it was made by La Dolores, so it was all right, for everyone knew how clean she and her husband, Melquiades, were and how carefully they tended their animals — just like her father and mother, old Gregorio and Seña Teófila, poor things, may they rest in peace.

As if under a compulsion, the Bacas continue to point out to him the folly of his ways and urge him, without expectation of success, to build up a savings account. Away from him, they laugh a little over his "ranch" and explain in detail its ridiculousness. Behind the words and the laughter lies the sense of the marvel, the greatest of all he has ever shown them. The Pendaries, Doña Marguerite's family, had given Rociada its name and founded the village of Gascón; for generations the Bacas had run their herds over those hills and valleys. Of them all, of the uncles, cousins, nephews, and nieces, not one remains along the Río Manuelitas. It is Canuto, the maverick out of Alabama, who has gone back, who owns land in the valley, and who brings them the news from Rociada.

At work in Doña Marguerite's house, he will retail the news — that Señor Juan is now blind but getting by nicely on his pension, being taken care of by his granddaughter Nieves, La Soledad's girl; that Pascual has finally been arrested; that Aurelia Jiménez has married Juan Lobato, and her eldest brother was knifed at the *baile* after the wedding; and that Josefita Gutiérrez has had a boy. Doña Marguerite will punctuate his stream of news at intervals with "*Va!*" or "*Válgame!*" or "That scrub!" or "Poor thing!" and then, in a slightly different tone and still without interrupting, tell him to clean the window sill properly before he puts down the cloth.

VII

The Convert

THE MOUNTAIN VILLAGES of New Mexico produce characters as marked as any to be found in rural New England, and as those villages are undisturbed by summer visitors, seldom touched even by writers seeking material, the characters are quite free of self-consciousness. They just are as they are. The Rociada area was no exception.

The girls growing up on the Baca ranch had a rich study in humanity available to them, even had they never visited in the surrounding villages. As I have already noted, anyone of consequence who came through Rociada put up at Doña Marguerite's, or at least stopped off there for a meal. Such visitors included the clergy, many of whom, like Father Mueller, had their quirks, Forest Service officials, surveyors, geologists, those who raised or dealt in cattle and sheep, an occasional artist from Santa Fe, with an easel on his pack mule and his paintbox on his saddle as they used to do in those days, a wide and hapchance assortment.

Also, part of the complex interweaving of ranch and

villages lay in visits. The Rociada people were forever dropping in. They did not visit empty-handed: the men brought trout, venison, occasional bear meat, and wild flowers, the women brought garden flowers, vegetables, or a bit of especially fine cookery. In the women's gifts there was often an element of innocent rivalry; to outcook Doña Marguerite, or to have a finer iris, an earlier rose, a later chrysanthemum than hers, if it could be done, was a real triumph.

The procedure of such visits followed pleasant custom. Something to eat, a glass of wine or a cup of coffee, a little talk, in the kitchen or in the living room according to the visitor's status, then a gift in return — a batch of *bizcochitos* or of American-style cookies, some of Doña Marguerite's splendid conserves, an article of clothing for a new baby, whatever was appropriate and available.

There are similar patterns of exchanges among simple people in many parts of the world, and to the outsider they look like barter, but they are not. They are an expression and reinforcement of warmth, and without affection there are neither visits nor presents. There was only one person who broke the general rule of exchange, the old, ragged blind woman, La Tulisa, who came begging as frankly as was possible among people who added touches of courtesy and grace to almost anything they did.

To the children, one of the astounding things about her was that, according to all reports, she had been neat and pretty once, long ago, when their Grandfather Pendaries had been the power in Rociada and walked the land with his sword cane and his handsome beard. She was old now, ragged, profoundly and anciently dirty, riding her burro that knew all the roads she wished to follow. She lived alone with her grandson Toribio, an infant, her chickens and her raggedy black dog. Somehow, and this too was astounding and unexplainable, she kept the grandchild clean and plump. The dog and the moth-eaten donkey were of a piece with herself.

She was grotesque, and she was also living legend. In those far days when she had been young, neat, and pretty, a small young woman with fine features and curly, rather light brown hair, a Baptist mission had established itself at Rociada. The people had depended for maintenance of their religion upon the occasional visits of the priest, in between these visits keeping up a continuity of rites in the church, and in their houses for the various crises of life and death, through prayer leaders learned in the hymns and prayers appropriate to all occasions.

The Baptists brought them the active, constant presence of a minister and in addition offered free schooling for those who wanted it. No one remembers just why Tulisa became their star convert, but she did, to the point that she moved into the mission to live. Others among the Rociada people swayed toward Protestantism, how much from the beginning of new belief, how much from curiosity and out of courtesy to newcomers who offered them many services and gifts of some value, such as clothing, it is impossible to tell.

The missionaries had no equipment for teaching a blind woman to read and write, but she learned a good deal of English and memorized a quantity of hymns, prayers,

Bible passages, and educative materials, thus sharpening a naturally excellent memory. The Baptists, a married couple, prized her dearly. A convert such as that, attractive, bright, appealing, touching, is a jewel in any mission's crown.

The mission was doing well; it began to look as if Protestantism would be established in Rociada. M. Pendaries decided to take action. He went to the Archbishop, and the Archbishop sent a counter-mission of Jesuits. As so often happens, the invading, active church stung the old, entrenched one into life. People came to the mission less and less. The coup de grâce was given when, even under the couple's guardianship, living in their house, Tulisa became pregnant and in due course was delivered of a daughter. She claimed she had been assaulted, and being blind, had no idea who had done it; local opinion put the finger on one of the ranch's best workmen, a handsome devil in his youth. That was the end of it. Sadly the missionaries moved out, the more sadly because their favorite chose to stay behind, which meant that she returned promptly to the Roman fold.

She changed over with a vengeance. That same memory that had enabled her to learn the Baptist rituals served her in mastering the *alabados,* the old Spanish hymns of praise with their haunting, almost Moorish melodies, the prayers and litanies, the Latin passages along with the Spanish, necessary for lay Catholic worship. She led the prayer in church, and was especially sought after for the rites required by doctrine and by custom for the *velorios,* the all-night watches over the dead.

Nor did she stop there. Most of the people of that region belonged to the order commonly known as "Penitentes," more properly *Los Hermanos de la Luz,* "The Brothers of the Light." The organization is something of a secret society, a genuine brotherhood much maligned in popular belief and newspaper figments. It is probably a local evolution out of the Third Order of Saint Francis, and it featured, until the present Archbishop took it in hand and brought it under control, an extreme of the flagellation so common among the sixteenth-century Spaniards who conquered New Mexico.

The principal ritual of the cult goes on during Lent, not in the churches as a usual thing, but in starkly plain, blank-walled chapels called *moradas.* It is guarded against the uninitiated, and as a rule women have no active part in it. The climax comes on Good Friday with the re-enactment of the Crucifixion — but they do not, as ignorant outsiders seem to believe, actually crucify anyone. Proscribed by the Catholic Church for generations, the cult nonetheless flourished among thousands of the mountain people, a form of super-devotion, an inner church, the extreme antithesis to Protestantism.

Being a leader of prayer in ordinary, public worship did not mean holding a formal position; someone simply acquired a reputation of knowing all the words and procedures and doing them well, and then was employed by common consent for the various occasions as they arose. The prayer leader among the Penitentes held definite office, with the title of *rezador,* and had to master a considerable corpus of special hymns and rituals. Not long before La

Tulisa's grandson was born the then *rezador* died, and there was trouble finding a competent replacement for him. Finally the Hermano Mayor, the head of the local organization, took the unprecedented step of appointing La Tulisa, a woman. Her long route back from the mission days could not possibly have taken her farther.

The Baca children found her grotesque, fascinating, and a bit frightening. Pino had taken part occasionally in Penitente rituals, the rest of the family stayed away from them. The girls' knowledge of the cult was vague, their impression of it colored by the sound, in the Lenten nights, of distant chanting and the eerie twining of a flute. The blind woman's part in all that set her apart, threw over her an aura of association with penances beyond imagining. This blended with the known picture of her as a kneeling figure, a slender bundle with the small oval of her head above it, entirely cased in a black shawl, by the altar in the church and in the lamp and candle light beside a bier. There was about her an atmosphere of worship, pain, and sorrow, in addition to dirt and rags, combined with which her habitual cheerfulness only made her more incongruous.

Her religious activities and her chickens earned her a minimal income, which she supplemented with charity. At regular intervals she would ride her burro to the back porch of the big house, the baby in front of her on the animal's withers, the dog trailing alongside. She came empty-handed. Doña Marguerite would set a chair for her on the porch, as she was too dirty to ask inside, give her some refreshment, and talk with her long enough to sustain the fiction of a social visit. If the girls were on hand they would come out, keeping a little distance from her, making conversation and studying her. Then their mother would give her her gift, and she would make her way back to the burro, mount, thwack it with a stick, and go along on her sightless rounds to Upper Rociada and Gascón.

The burro's name was Kitty, which she rendered as "La Keetty." That name was all that remained of her education and her mission days.

VIII

Miss Eufemia's Nose

AS NEARLY AS Consuelo can remember, she was nine when Miss Eufemia came to Rociada. If Consuelo was nine, then that would make Carmen eleven and Pepita seven. The three older children were by then in boarding school or college.

Life in the mid-nineteen-twenties had a timelessness that makes it difficult for my wife and her sisters to place the events of their childhood in order or to date them. That life has so completely ended that when they talk about it now, it is as if they were recalling some far-off legendary period. Each detail is jewel-clear, complete in itself, and part of the larger pattern that is like a bird's-eye view of time, spread out flat and unchanging. If, as children, they had been given to such reflections, they would have thought that their governess, Miss Eufemia, was to be the means by which they could continue that charmed life forever; yet, strangely, it was through her failure, which they helped to bring about, that change, inexorable and unalterable, began.

Up to the year before, the children had been taught by their parents. Both had more than enough to do, and their teaching was, of necessity, sporadic. As Carmen began to get leggy and approach her teens, they realized that the three wild little girls needed to be taught not only reading, writing, and arithmetic but some of the accomplishments of young ladies; also, that they needed a teacher who would bring them up speaking correct English and Spanish, and introduce them to French. The school in Rociada village would not serve. It was a one-room affair, in which the local young squirmed on wooden benches and achieved a mild literacy. The duration of their schooling depended on their own or their parents' persistence. It was not considered a serious deficiency if the graduates of that school, reasoning from the Spanish *esposo* and *esposa,* said "hosband" indiscriminately for man and wife, or used the pronoun "she" in reference to any noun that in Spanish takes *"ella."*

The year before, the Bacas had tried to solve the problem of the children's education by uprooting themselves to winter in Las Vegas. The little girls were not happy over this move. Rociada was their domain. Their parents were firm, their father rather awe-inspiring, but the girls were allowed plenty of freedom. Discipline was warmed by love, and in both discipline and love was anchored security. The workmen and servants — all Spanish-Americans except for Canuto — indulged them. They had the riverbanks, the wide valley, the forested mountainsides to roam, the villages to visit, the barns and corrals to explore. They had the rich long grass and countless flowers in summer, the shining heavy snows in winter. It was not easy for them to get used to the confinement of city life and to the big classrooms full of strange children.

Carmen and Pepita got along fairly well, although they found the big schools far from ideal. Carmen was naturally confident, and Pepita, even at six, possessed a self-contained independence. Consuelo was the one most in need of support. Strangers made her timid; away from home she faced each new situation half anticipating failure. Consuelo's class was presided over by a Miss Coombs. She was a mean woman, who brought to Las Vegas all of a lower-middle-class Middle Westerner's resentment of and hostility toward the exotic characteristics of the Spanish Southwest. What prejudices were not native to her she was quick to acquire from the Texans who eternally infiltrate New Mexico. To her, this child with jet-black hair and unusually large brown eyes was just another little Mexican, except that, improperly, she was a well-dressed, well-fed little Mexican with an unconsciously proud carriage, who spoke correct, unlocalized English with only the faintest occasional Spanish intonations. It further offended Miss Coombs to know that Consuelo's father was a man of eminence and authority, whom people, even those she would call Americans, spoke of as a possible candidate for governor.

Outwardly proud, inwardly unsure of herself, Consuelo missed a simple question early in the school year. Miss Coombs pounced on her, and continued to pounce unflaggingly, week after week. Misery spread over the girl's life, taking out the light, killing the colors, changing it absolutely. Mornings were for feeling sick to one's stomach and crying quietly on the way to school; the infinite hours before school let out were for hoping desperately to be overlooked; the rest of the day was for trying not to remember that morning must come again.

The children obviously were not receiving the kind of education their parents had in mind. Moreover, of their playmates many spoke the slurred New Mexico dialect of Spanish, and others equally dialectic English. Everything being taken into consideration, the experiment was not a success. To the joy of all of them, the Bacas returned to the ranch in the spring, and Don José and Doña Marguerite set about finding a suitable governess.

This was no simple matter. Women of the kind they sought were generally appalled at the idea of going to a ranch in the wilds of New Mexico. They anticipated Indians with scalping knives, cowboys shooting promiscuously into the air, rattlesnakes, and Gila monsters. Those who grasped that Rociada was a Spanish-American community visualized murderous Mexicans, each with a serape drawn across his mouth and chin, and beady black eyes glittering under the brim of a straw sombrero. Don José turned to old Mexico. Through friends in the American Legation in Mexico City, he found out about Miss Eufemia Sotomayor, a decayed gentlewoman living near Guadalajara. Negotiations were carried on by mail, and she was engaged sight unseen.

From the outset, the family spoke of her as Miss, and not as Señorita, because Don José insisted that the children's basic language be English. She came of an excellent family that had been ruined in the series of revolutions that followed the overthrow of Porfirio Díaz. She was half French, and spoke both French and Spanish with elegance; her English, as it turned out, was strongly accented and a trifle uncertain.

The children awaited their governess's coming with mixed feelings. Their father had arranged one room as a classroom for them. There was a definite quality of school to that, something far more regular and confining than when their parents were teaching them, but at least it was their own classroom, far from Las Vegas, safe from strangers. From their older brother and sisters, and from their various cousins in and around Las Vegas, they had come to realize that there were kinds of knowledge one really had to acquire. They had even experienced moments of wanting to learn. Above all, there was the excitement of a new person coming to live with them. She might prove to be fun; certainly, under their own roof, under their parents' eyes, there would be no need to fear her.

Miss Eufemia arrived in the fall. The Bacas made an occasion of it, the whole family driving by car to Las Vegas to meet her at the station. The thing that impressed Consuelo and her sisters most, the thing they always remember first when they tell about this happening, was Miss Eufemia's trunk. It was huge, the biggest anyone in Rociada had ever seen. Pascual Orozco hauled the trunk to the ranch in his wagon. Four strong men — Juan Grande, Juan Chico, Canuto, and Señor Juan — were needed to wrestle the trunk upstairs to Miss Eufemia's room, where it remained, locked, enormous, mysterious. No one ever saw it open; the only clue the family ever had to its contents was the fine, costly jewelry the governess sometimes wore. Everyone speculated; everyone still does.

Miss Eufemia herself was a large dignified woman with gray in her black hair. On the day of her arrival, she wore a plum-colored dress and an impressive, elaborate hat. She was handsome, but the regularity of her features was marred by a curious blunt tip to her nose. It caught the children's attention instantly. By the time they had ridden the sixty-five miles back to Rociada, the tip of Miss Eufemia's nose had become as important to them as the trunk — a fascinating oddity, something that one ought to *do* something about, although they could not imagine what.

Miss Eufemia was accustomed to the empty spaces and the wide-scattered haciendas of Mexico, and therefore not surprised or dismayed by the remoteness of Rociada. The luxurious touring car in which she was driven showed her at the start that although the Bacas were North Americans, they maintained the style one expected of *hacendados* of good family. The two-story ranchhouse, with its roof pitched steeply enough to handle heavy snows, its long porches front and back, was alien, and so was the free use of logs and bark-covered slabs in the lesser structures, but the general layout — corrals, bunkhouse, outbuildings, and barns — made a familiar and adequate picture. She surmised that the adobe villages of Rociada and Upper Rociada were dependent upon the ranch, but later she was surprised to discover that the villagers owned their own homes, that some of them had their own farming land, and that they were free to come and go as they pleased. The revolutions in Mexico, especially the uprising led by Calles, were bringing about a similarly anarchic condition there, but here it did not seem to lead to ruin.

What Miss Eufemia was not at all prepared for, what she had with great difficulty to learn, was that her charges, to whom she was to impart the feminine accomplishments and unexacting education of her own upbringing, were not three Spanish girls, reared according to a rigid social tradition that derives ultimately from the Moors, but three little Americans. New Mexico had in it a great deal of old Spain, but it was old Spain merged with the still lively Western frontier and conditioned accordingly. The girls were tomboys. When their energy was held in too long, the pressure became more than they could contain. Together, on their home grounds, they were an untamed little tribe.

Miss Eufemia's teaching was not too hard to absorb. She was not strong in arithmetic; their problems were prepared for them by their father and, though worked out under the governess's supervision, carried the aura of his authority. With a grammar open before her, Miss Eufemia could give adequate instruction in English. The children studied some history and read a good deal of poetry aloud from books in their parents' library. They learned French and improved their Spanish mostly in the course of extensive religious instruction, and through the children's songs Miss Eufemia taught them when they went for a walk in the afternoons and on mornings when they were too restless to sit still. Their conception of a walk was most unladylike. As soon as they were out of the house, their world spread before them, and they raced into it. There was no way Miss Eufemia could make them come back. Her only control over the extent of their wandering lay in the fact that she carried the lunch. The children never went on an expedition without a lunch. Eventually, appetite pulled them back to where Miss Eufemia awaited them, and it was then that she taught them the songs they loved, such as "Sur le pont d'Avignon," "Il était une bergère," and "El Torito."

Miss Eufemia's greatest enthusiasm was reserved for the periods of instruction in the graceful arts. The girls were musical. They took kindly to short periods at the piano, learning to play by ear entirely, as Miss Eufemia could not read notes. Much more time went into painting water colors. In the shattered society of Miss Eufemia's past, she had enjoyed some reputation as a painter. She offered one of her paintings as a prize for reciting the Lord's Prayer all the way through in French. Consuelo broke down on the first try, partly because her gaze became riveted on Miss Eufemia's nose, but she made it the second time without coaching. The prize was an oil painting of bluebirds sitting on a fence, with forget-me-nots in the foreground and a pinkish evening sky with cupids' heads floating among topaz clouds. Consuelo thought this truly wonderful. It was a proud thing to have a real picture, the kind you put in a frame and cover with glass, all your own and given to you by the artist herself.

It was in connection with the painting lessons that the first real conflict between Miss Eufemia and her pupils developed. Carmen, surprisingly, painted the way she was shown, but Consuelo, for all her admiration of her prize picture, was unable to resist her own stronger tastes when the brush was in her hand. She preferred orange bluebirds to blue ones, and, loving a good red at any time, saw no reason not to paint the sky that color. Invariably, she turned away from the soft tints her teacher considered aesthetic and suitable, and chose instead purer, more vigorous tones, with a definite leaning toward the primary colors. Miss Eufemia found her work disturbing, unrealistic, and harsh.

Pepita was intrigued by her sister's style. One warm day, a projection of Indian summer into the late autumn, Pepita was occupied with a composition involving a central mass of violets. She painted as she did everything else, in a self-contained way, isolated in her absorption, wanting no interference. She had made a pool of clear rich yellow in her pan; against the white enamel it glowed like a daffodil in sunlight. The living color spoke to her. She wanted to transfer it to her picture, and since the violets were the dominant element, she set about painting them yellow. On paper, the color thinned and lost life. She dug her small brush into the pigment, getting a thicker mixture, building it on the flowers. She worked on, lost in the technical problem and the excitement of her intention. When Miss Eufemia spoke at her shoulder, asking with disapproval why she painted her violets yellow, Pepita was unpleasantly startled, and answered brashly, "Because they're lemons."

The two other girls laughed, and Miss Eufemia was upset. That evening, she asked Don José to discipline the children by making up an extra, difficult problem in arithmetic for the next day, which he did. The girls worked on the problem together and solved it correctly, but not in the way Don José had explained to the governess. She pointed out to them that their method was wrong, but she could not get around the fact that their answer was correct. The unorthodoxy so troubled her that she suspended the arithmetic lesson and took them for walk.

That day, when they ate their lunches, the girls sat close to her. They sang songs as usual. By common consent, without anything being said, without anything specific being formulated in their minds, they deliberately held their sandwiches in such a way that jam dripped on her dress.

As winter kept them more indoors, the classroom hours grew more disorderly. The children twined themselves about their governess affectionately but with a total lack of respect, took liberties with her, occasionally pushed pieces of paper into her hair or ears. At times when she had her pupils all seated properly in a row, their rapt attention meant simply that they were contemplating that fascinating blunt end of her nose.

They were fond of Miss Eufemia, and that fondness, freely shown, was one of the things that baffled her attempts at discipline. She was lonely, she wanted the affection they readily gave, but they bewildered her and she had no idea where to draw a line. Often enough she held their interest, but at times she bored them, and as the memory of the school at Las Vegas faded, the very fact of their classroom irked them. They were obliged to torment her, through the law of nature that requires children to explore and develop to the full any advantage over an adult, just as a stream must explore and develop any weakness in its containing banks.

When the rumpus grew too great or the insults to her person were too obvious, Miss Eufemia would threaten to tell the little girls' father. Then there would be an instantaneous change. The girls would be on their knees, pleading, promising, angelic, with their black hair, their large eyes, their fine hands outstretched — three outrageously charming little hypocrites putting into the drama of penitence and reform all of their Latin heritage. Miss Eufemia would relent, and there would follow a second satisfying drama of reconciliation.

When spring came in full force and the pale blue mountain iris began to dot the meadows, Miss Eufemia went back to Mexico and the girls were turned loose. Emilie, Pino, and Marie came home from boarding school and college. Summer was a spacious time of complete freedom, enlivened by the visits of assorted cousins and the older children's school friends — Easterners, in the main — who had strange, interesting customs and lived in a state of surprise at the most ordinary things.

The three younger children were not oppressed by the thought that in the fall Miss Eufemia would return and school would start again. They had, really, no objection to her; on the whole, they would be glad to see her. Overshadowing everything else was the fact that she was bringing her nephew with her, a boy whose parents had been killed in one of the Mexican revolutions. They talked about him all through the summer, making plans. His name was Ernesto. Miss Eufemia had told them that he was dark, and tall for his age, and that he would be thirteen, a year older than Carmen, so they imagined him to be on the order of their father and Pino, who between them represented the acme of manhood and good looks. Ernesto, especially since he was a Mexican, would be very much a man — *muy hombre*. He would be these things scaled down to the girls' size and age, living with them at Rociada. They were impatient for his arrival.

The big car brought Miss Eufemia and her nephew to Rociada in the middle of September. Miss Eufemia had a collection of presents for the girls — little Mexican baskets, tiny glass figures, costume dolls, and other enchanting miniature objects of the kind Mexico abounds in. Introductions were made. The girls greeted the boy formally, hardly able to form an impression of him in all the business of gifts and salutations, the handling of luggage and the showing to rooms. When the fine confusion of the arrival had died down, the three girls found themselves in the yard, standing in a quarter circle, contemplating the newcomer.

He was tall and dark, and he was weedy; on his pale thin face was the look of delicate health and of the student. Considering him, they saw timidity. It did not occur to them to wonder whether this was innate or came from the strangeness and loneliness of this new land and the new faces. They simply felt that he met neither the Spanish nor the American conception of a man. His clothes were citified and extremely neat; he wore a dark blue chesterfield and black silk gloves. Although he was so warmly dressed, he shivered slightly in the cool of the evening. Standing there, exchanging a few exploratory words with him, they all knew that they rejected him.

Ernesto had polished manners — the full, formal politeness that survives intact in Mexico but north of the border has become truncated and hastened. He was grave and well behaved. He conversed thoughtfully with grownups; grownups liked him. As far as the girls were concerned, he was of no use. He did not like to get mussed or dirty. When he went outdoors in the sharp October air, his aunt wrapped him up to an extent the girls thought ridiculous; when the snows came, she bundled him even more warmly in scarves, sweaters, jackets, and gloves; it was a wonder he could move at all. He showed no desire to get rid of any of these garments.

Ernesto had had regular schooling. He was training himself for a profession. His education had gone far beyond anything the girls could follow, and it must have reached, if not exceeded, the limits of Miss Eufemia's knowledge. He liked to study. He spent long hours at his books, fulfilling the assignments he and his aunt worked out between them.

Partly to bedevil him, partly because one *had* to attack so unnatural a mode of life, the girls would stand outside his window, teasing and begging him to come out. Sometimes they succeeded, but he did not understand or care for their play; he did not, for instance, like to climb about the long, dim hayloft of the big barn, trying to kill rats with a baling hook. More often, Miss Eufemia chased the little girls away from Ernesto's window, or else, after a short time, with the light brilliant on the snow and so many things to be done before the sun went behind the mountains, they gave up and left him to study in peace.

Soon after he came, Consuelo and Carmen fixed him an apple-pie bed. Ernesto made no mention of it. They tried two or three more tricks on him, with the same lack of results. Increasingly, they let him alone. The workmen took pity on him and invited him to ride with them as they went about their business on fine days; he rode easily, as a Mexican should. They could not have been much company for him; he must have found their speech barbarous and their manners rough, and while they were undoubtedly respectful, their lack of the deference he was accustomed to expect from their kind in his own country — for example, the entire freedom with which they called him by his first name — must have troubled him.

The girls neither knew nor wondered what Ernesto thought of them, nor did they give any thought to what memories he might carry with him of tragedy and loss. He told no tales, made no overtures, kept silence. He had, in fact, a courage to which they did not have the key. He adapted himself to loneliness, in an appalling land where the first snow flies in November and the snows continue to pile up as though summer were over forever. As the cold months went by, the three girls became used to Ernesto, and he, presumably, became used to them.

Even in the high mountains of New Mexico winter does end. But spring comes hesitantly there: a few warm days, a great melting of snow and rushing of streams, and then it withdraws before new snow and new freezing. By the middle of April one knows that winter is in full retreat, even if not yet routed. It is a time when people soften, become brighter, and look about them, pleased, feeling the warm sun in the afternoon and seeing the green returning.

Consuelo's birthday, in April, was made into an extra-special occasion that year, merely because Carmen was feeling creative and had worked out a pageant for it. The girls were to be princesses and Consuelo was to be crowned queen. Miss Eufemia helped to make the crown. Ernesto consented to be the prince and crown the queen. The pageant was performed with the household, including the servants, as audience. Ernesto, in a sash and cloak, played his part splendidly. He had gravity and grace; he knew how to make imaginary royalty seem important. The crown was made of gold paper, shining, and adorned with early crocuses and a few geraniums and other flowers from Doña Marguerite's array of potted plants. Ernesto's deep bow at the very end was magnificent. Consuelo loved wearing her crown afterward while they had refreshments and her birthday cake.

Because Ernesto had really shone in the pageant, the girls became warmer and more friendly toward him; most of their harrying had dropped away long since, from lack of interest. He still kept to his study hours, but he spent more time with them and was probably more at ease himself. He wanted to practise English as much as possible, and English was their mother tongue, but there were so many things that one could say better in Spanish than in English; there were, for that matter, so many things about the ranch for which the English word, when he and the little girls knew it, sounded clumsy and unreal. They talked together in a free mixture of the two languages, with occasionally a word or phrase of French.

Ernesto told them something about himself and about life in Mexico; his accounts, from the point of view of one of the girls' own age or near it, were richer, more vivid than his aunt's. They learned that he had brothers and sisters, and they caught some inkling, in the tone of his voice or in his expression when he spoke of his parents, of what being an orphan meant. He mentioned his parents seldom, as a matter of fact, and although the girls would have liked to know more, they did not press him. For the first time they felt honest sympathy for him and realized that his reticences were not mere withdrawal. They saw, and appreciated, his character, even though vaguely.

With May came the beginning of real spring. The children were restless, their boiling points lower than ever. One evening, Pepita brought a box containing three horny toads up to bed with her. She had caught them, she explained, because Señor Juan had told her that a horny toad, if you stuck a cigarette into its mouth, would smoke. She wanted to find out if this statement was true, but she didn't see how they could get a cigarette — not until the next day, anyway. The two older girls thought that the toads should be put to good use right away. Ernesto was one of them now — it was almost an automatic act to put the toads in his bed and surprise him, as each of them had been surprised by the two others at one time or another. They went to his room. By the time they had put two of the toads under the covers, they were in a state of high suppressed giggles. They could not resist putting the third one in Miss Eufemia's bed.

Ernesto went to bed half an hour later. He did what any of the three girls would have done — got rid of the toads, and made no sign. Miss Eufemia's reaction was less controlled, and Don José learned of the trick.

The next morning, he spoke severely to his daughters, pointing out how disrespectful, rude, childish, and inhospitable the trick had been. To the children, this was genuine punishment. They were truly sorry, they apologized to him and to their governess, and they resolved solemnly to be good.

Spring came on full blast; the short time of studying that remained to them seemed like eternity. The sun was hot, the flowers were out, the great flocks of sheep were moving up from the low country, accompanied by little gay, frantic lambs. One morning when all outdoors was calling the children, Miss Eufemia read history to her pupils. She had let the girls gather around her; Carmen, toying uneasily with a blue crayon, sat on the arm of her chair. She could not take her eyes off Miss Eufemia's nose. The reading voice passed meaninglessly through her mind; the day teased through the open window. In a sort of compulsive madness, while the other two watched in admiration and alarm, she pressed the dull point of the crayon against the fascinating, flattened tip and turned it, making a clear blue spot.

Miss Eufemia rushed from the room in tears, and once again the girls confronted their father's anger. Doña Marguerite also let them know how shocked she was. The governess was too hurt for good relations to be restored in the usual prompt way. The classroom days ended with everyone subdued. Ernesto withdrew from the girls a little, as they themselves would have done had he thus affronted a member of their family.

Don José and Doña Marguerite agreed that Miss Eufemia's usefulness had come to an end; no matter how good their daughters' intentions might be, if she returned for another season, she could not manage them. At Las Vegas a convent boarding school had been opened by the Sisters of Loretto, who taught the things that the Bacas wanted their children to learn. There was no danger there of a repetition of Miss Coombs, and a couple of the Sisters were French. Carmen and Consuelo would be old enough to go there in the fall; Pepita could follow in a year or two.

With the approach of summer, Miss Eufemia departed for good, with her nose, with the trunk that no one had ever seen unlocked, and with Ernesto. Her parting with the girls was frankly emotional on both sides. Consuelo wept. Ernesto was, as ever, restrained, and his restraint affected the girls; even so, at the last moment, in the face of the real evidences of their regret, he became friendly and warm, behind his formality. Whether he was glad, relieved, or sorry to be shut of Rociada, no one could tell.

The car disappeared down a road newly turned dusty

after the spring mud. With it went the last hope of a life indefinitely contained within the circle that surrounded Rociada like an enchantment. In September, two of the girls would be leaving home, and from then on they would be away for longer and longer periods of time, the gap in the circle becoming a little wider and then a little wider, until there was no more circle — until there was nothing at all but the memory, which made one laugh and cry, of things that seemed to have existed not in this present life but in some far-distant, irretrievable time.

IX

A Job and a Lunch

THE MOST IMPORTANT happenings of our lives — those meetings and combinations that uproot us from what we thought were to be our homes and set us down to live in the most unlikely places, that make our fortunes or break us, that result in the begetting of our children — occur as a result of haphazard, often minor, chances. By similarly slight chances, other meetings and combinations fail to occur.

I confront the curious thought that a very slight rearrangement of events would have resulted in my meeting the girl who is now my wife not in the course of the Santa Fe Fiesta in 1936 but in the mid-twenties, when she and her family still lived on her father's great ranch. When from that I go on to speculate as to what effect this earlier meeting would have had in hastening, delaying, or preventing an ultimate development for which I am profoundly grateful, my mind rocks. The attempt to consider what alteration in the chain of years, what ramifications of new causes, would have led to what results confronts one with the whole mechanism of destiny and leads one to the edge of the abyss of infinity.

Though it is impossible to proceed very far by such speculation, it is easy to imagine the meeting in the mid-twenties that did not take place. I was then just entering the postgraduate practice of archaeology. In the pursuit of that odd career, I might just as well have been sent to the Pecos Ruin, in the southern foothills of the Sangre de Cristo Mountains, in New Mexico, as to the desert wastes of northeastern Arizona, where I actually was sent. Then, instead of being sent out from the main excavation to scout a far-reaching system of barren canyons, I would have been sent north from Pecos, up into the mountains. As the valley of the Pecos River itself had already been well studied, I would have entered the next river system to the east, and so in due course during the second or third summer have come out into the achingly beautiful valley of Rociada.

Once there, I would have drawn out my stay as long as possible, although indications of archaeological sites are almost nil. The rich pastures and the small, hardy, close-clustered farms along the fast clear stream that runs down the center of the valley, the settlements of reddish-brown adobe houses, and the forested, rugged yet gentle mountains that, for all their height, seem protective rather than brooding make all comers want to linger.

Unquestionably, I would have called upon Don José Baca. Young and brash, I would not have hesitated to present myself to the principal person of that isolated land. I would have been curious, in any case, to take a look at a *seigneurie* that was more like something out of past time than like anything one would expect to find in the United States of the prohibition era. I would also, of course, have heard of the Bacas' open hospitality.

Then, too, I would most probably have heard that the son, Pino, also just out of college, was quite a lad, and it would certainly have occurred to me that he could put me in the way of obtaining a supply of local whiskey. I can see myself, the typical pup field scientist — high-laced boots, Boy Scout hat, small spurs, and all — riding up to the steps before the long veranda of the big high-shouldered ranchhouse.

On the veranda, on the right days of that second or third summer in the Southwest, I would have found two extremely pretty little girls, one about ten, one about eight, dressed in the blue denim ranch clothes that were then so strange to Easterners. They would have been seated in rocking chairs that were much too big for them, rocking industriously.

I never saw those rocking chairs, but they have been described to me. They had long, solid, strongly curved rockers. Behind each chair, on the rockers, lay a good-sized wooden keg, which rolled forward to the legs of the chair and then back almost to the ends of the curved rockers as the girls swung the chairs. Keeping the heavy kegs going just right, so that they did not bang or fall off, required a technique that was achieved by long practice.

What I would have made of this scene at first sight, heaven knows. Eventually, I would have learned that the girls were aging Pino's whiskey. For this work, he paid them five cents an hour. That the older of the two girls could be my future wife would certainly never have crossed my mind.

For any definite job that their elders asked them to do, the girls expected to be paid. What was unusual about this keg-rocking, from their point of view, was that it was the only job they had ever had for which they did not demand additional payment in the form of a lunch. For an activity of any duration, whether pleasure or work, a lunch was absolutely essential, but in this case the contract was with their brother, not their parents. Also, the work was done right at the house, and if they felt hungry, they could go the kitchen and pester their mother or the servants for cookies.

Living in partial isolation, Don José's three younger children developed tribal patterns of their own, including patterns for work. If the work permitted sitting, they took along their chairs — three child-sized rockers, which they had already outgrown but to which they were devoted. They also liked to take their quilts, which originally had covered them in their cribs, to sit or lie on or to wear as shawls, and their miniature suitcases, to hold their lunch, and, whenever possible, one or more dolls. Don José and Doña Marguerite permitted the paraphernalia, just as they accepted the demand for pay, without objection and without visible amusement.

There were some chores that could hardly be turned into paid fun. The post office that served the three villages of the valley was at the ranch; Don José was postmaster. The mail came through daily by buggy from Sápello reaching Rociada any time between two in the afternoon and nightfall, according to the state of the road — dry, muddy, washed out, or deep in snow — and how long Amadeo Lobato stopped to talk when he came through Peñasco or at ranches along the way. It was the whole household's duty to receive the mail and have the outgoing letters canceled and ready. Whoever was free attended to this. No one saw anything out of the way in having the mail handled by two or three little girls ranging in age from eight to twelve, or, for that matter, by Canuto. Canuto could not read well, but he had a good hand with the cancellation and postmark.

Don José maintained the commissary as part of his ranching operation. Originally for outfitting his herders before they went on the ranges to take care of his flocks or his cattle, the commissary had evolved into a well-equipped store, competing with Tomás Lobato's store in Rociada village. The children took brief turns at helping behind the counter. Consuelo especially liked to sell cut plug. The tobacco came in long, dark slabs, which one cut to proper length with a sort of guillotine. The blade came down with a little thump and a crunch, making a clean-edged cut. She enjoyed the feel of the machine, the sense of its accuracy and force. Occasionally, business got so brisk that the children's help was needed for more than casual moments. Then they drove their customary bargain with their father before they went to work. Tending store permitted only the fewest accessories, hardly more than a doll perched on a shelf.

The children's primary business, of course, was play.

Doña Marguerite's mother had never quite reconciled herself to the frontier life of the mountains in which her husband had created his domain. She had kept her daughter close by her side, holding her to a confined, indoor life. Doña Marguerite, rebelling against that upbringing, let her daughters run free.

Ordinarily they did not go to the villages without an escort. This seems not to have been a matter of protecting them so much as of propriety and convention. When they went riding — not playing on the burros in one of the pastures but really riding — again ordinarily, but not always, they had a *vaquero* with them. On foot, they set out for wherever they pleased, with or without dolls, quilts, and other equipment, but always with a lunch. The pine forests, the scratching, clothes-tearing tangles of oak brush on some of the mountainsides, the branch canyons, each threaded with its little brook, the meadows, the swimming holes in the river were all theirs. Work was occasional and incidental. At times the children's help was genuinely needed, but parental indulgence was often involved in the arrangement, and work provided a substitute for the more varied activities possible where the young of many families run together.

A job that typifies many, and that Consuelo remembers extra clearly, was helping to fill the silo. One afternoon during a period when the ranch was temporarily shorthanded, Don José sent for the three girls to come to the commissary for a conference. Carmen took a seat on a sack of beans, Consuelo on a ten-pound bucket of lard. Their father picked up Pepita and set her on the battered high wooden counter, so that as he sat at his rolltop desk he could see them all. He always handled the question of their employment gravely, making terms with them as if they were adults. This time, he explained that Juan Grande had not come to work and that he thought the three of them could take Juan Grande's place inside the silo to stamp down the ensilage as it poured in. He offered to pay them, collectively, seven and a half cents an hour.

The children asked for nine cents, arguing that seven and a half could not be divided equally among three. After a little more talk, Don José agreed. The children hurried off to the house to get ready. Since they would be in one place the whole afternoon, they could bring all their goods — chairs, dolls, quilts, and suitcases full of lunch.

The cornstalks were fed into a machine that chopped them and drove them with a blower through a great, snakelike metal tube that spewed them into the silo from above. It made a strange, almost alarming noise. The silo had a vertical row of small square unglazed windows that closed with a sliding wooden cover. The children peered through one of these openings at the inside of the big wooden tower. It looked dusky and mysterious. They were boosted in through the third window from the bottom and tumbled down, landing on a heap of chopped, dusty, damp, sugary cornstalks. The blower started going too soon, shooting a stream of wind and ensilage on Consuelo's head. The corn fragments stung like hail. The girls wrapped their quilts around them against the artificial storm, arranged their belongings, and fell to work at trampling.

It had, inevitably, to become a game. They decided to

be Indians, Pueblo Indians, and the name of their pueblo was Maíz, or Corn. As Indians, they danced, jumped, and ran around. The game took form, with parts for the dolls and uses for the chairs. It was a game, a dance, and a play. They kept trampling and jumping, they were having great fun, and for this they were being paid nine cents an hour.

The ensilage rose steadily higher, lifting them with it. After an hour, Consuelo suddenly remembered the suitcases. The quilts they were wearing, the dolls they were carrying, the chairs they kept using, but the suitcases, which they had put aside until they should want their lunch and quite forgotten about, were buried out of sight. All three girls started screaming. Their father had the machine stopped and climbed in in a hurry. When he found out what the trouble was, he dug up the suitcases. Then he spoke to the girls rather sharply. They ought not to be so careless, he told them. What if it had been one of them? The sequence of ideas was illogical, but they had just given him a good fright.

In due course, the girls ate their lunches, mixed with ensilage, which gave jelly sandwiches and native cheese a new, interesting flavor. The last of the cornstalks went, finally, through the machine into the silo, and the adventure was over. It had been quite the most exciting work they had ever done. Pepita found that one of her doll's shoes was hopelessly lost. She wanted to cry, but she didn't.

Don José took them back to the commissary; paid them off, with proper formality, from the till, not from his pocket; and gave them store cookies, in case they were still hungry, which they were. They went back to the house, trailing their belongings, hot, dirty in a new, corn-scented manner, tired, rich, eating cookies, and speculating as to which cow would one day eat the doll's shoe.

It was perhaps that same year or the year after (there is no way to fix anything that happened in those secluded years in a sure chronological order) that the little girls had the job of herding rams, which is the other employment Consuelo remembers most vividly. Don José's father, who at one time owned a hundred thousand head of sheep, started out with the hardy native breed. His son had improved the strain, especially with Rambouillets, until the flocks had reached a high quality. For further improvement, Don José brought in six pedigreed, blue-ribbon rams — beautiful, thick-fleeced, straight-backed, full-grown animals, with long, aquiline faces, wise eyes, and wonderfully curling horns.

Before putting the rams out on the range, he kept them for a while in a corral at the ranch, pasturing them nearby under special supervision. The three girls were enchanted with the beasts; quickly each selected and named a favorite. Carmen, in a burst of originality, named hers Wheatie, because he loved the green wheat she pulled and brought to him. The two younger girls had already given theirs more ordinary names — Angelico and Chico Grande. They admired their sister's imagination.

The rams' special herder and several of the other workmen went to a baptismal party at Peñasco, where they got drunk and took it into their heads to go visiting friends at Sápello. They stayed away for two days. Señor Juan could take care of the rams in the corral, but for the moment there was no one to herd them. During the first of these two days, the rams were pastured on the green pure grass of the Bacas' yard. The girls were detailed to keep them out of the flowerbeds. They were so entranced at this opportunity to be with the rams all they wanted, to feel their fleece, pet their foreheads, and run exploring hands over their magnificent horns, that it did not occur to them to demand pay. They stayed in the yard all day, except when they ran outside to gather long grass and wheat, which they distributed with rank favoritism toward their respective pets.

Six healthy rams can graze down a fair-sized yard pretty fast. Toward the middle of the second morning, when there was no sign of the missing workmen, Don José asked the girls to take the animals to pasture. This was clearly a job, so the usual bargaining ensued.

As there might be some need for running, the children carried only dolls, quilts, and a lunch. The rams knew the way, so they herded easily enough. The girls walked quietly behind and alongside the animals, trailing or cradling their dolls. They watched their flock until time for their noon meal; then they went home.

Before going back to the pasture, they demanded another lunch, and got a big one of cookies and divinity. Divinity consists principally of white of egg, sugar, corn syrup, vanilla, and chopped black walnuts. Then they returned to their charges, who received them graciously. Consuelo produced a length of blue ribbon, which she managed to attach, with a bow, to the horns of her favorite, Angelico. The other girls wished that they had thought of that.

The rams' business was eating. The girls knew that they should not interrupt it, and so they settled down in the shade of an oak clump to set up a social life for their dolls. Suddenly they heard, out in the field, a resounding smack. They started up. Angelico and one of the anonymous rams were fighting. The others shifted about uneasily, stamped, ruffled their nostrils, and looked threatening. The two combatants danced, lowered their heads, and charged each other with another crash. Then for a long time they stayed head to head, pushing each other, trampling the grass, and snorting.

The girls were terrified. In an instant the rams had become strange, their very appearance new and fearful. Carmen and Consuelo dropped their dolls Then they all turned and ran for the pines at the edge of the pasture. They each climbed high up in a tree to safety.

They stayed in the trees, trembling, and watched the fearful battle. The rams might kill each other. Or there might be a general melee and a gory aftermath. Consuelo and Carmen were torn by fear for their dolls, which lay by the oak clump much too near the scene of battle. Pepita had hung on to hers, but its dress had been torn and its arm scratched on its way up the tree. The children were thoroughly scared, a condition that was heightened by their sense of the dramatic, which even in their fright did not leave them.

Soon the two fighters lost interest in their quarrel and

fell to grazing. Everything became quiet. The rams looked familiar once more, and harmless. Hesitantly, the girls climbed down. They picked up their dolls, checked on their quilts and their lunch. Suddenly they were very hungry.

The rams had meant no harm, the girls argued. Perhaps they had really been playing; such magnificent creatures might easily be terrible in their play. Anyway, they were quiet now. Angelico had lost his ribbon. Consuelo did not say so, but she no longer thought that a ribbon suited him. The girls opened their lunch. It seemed mean to eat all that divinity without letting their favorites have some, too. Tentatively, they approached the animals.

Wheatie, Angelico, and Chico Grande were used to eating out of the children's hands by that time. They had learned that what was brought to them thus was generally better than the provender underfoot. When the girls came up to them, hands outstretched, ready to run, if necessary, the rams raised their heads amicably. They found divinity delicious; they liked the cookies.

Fear dropped away. The girls were delighted. They felt that somehow they had conquered and tamed raging beasts. Love and pride of possession rose within them. They ate evenly, unselfishly, with their pets. Consuelo, feeling sorry for the three nameless rams, divided a cookie among them. Finally, everything in the box was gone. All was peaceful in the pasture. When the sun went low in the sky, they herded the rams home, contented, looking forward to their pay.

The following morning, Wheatie, Angelico, and Chico

Grande, several thousand dollars' worth of prize breeding stock, were found dead in the corral. The girls were heartbroken and bewildered. They mourned the rams and were deeply unhappy to see their father so upset. He questioned them, and when he learned what they had fed their three pets, he assumed a manner of agonized restraint. The previous year, the girls had successfully raised a lamb, starting it on a bottle. Their father asked if they had fed it divinity. They had. They had always shared fairly with it, after it was off the bottle. Don José explained certain facts about animals' diet to them, with the same restraint, but his heart was not in it.

That lamb — possibly because it was a native animal and because they started it off young — had thrived, on grass, cookies, divinity, whatever affection prompted them to give it. How could the children know, then, that a sudden feeding of exotic items would be too much for the effete, aristocratic newcomers? How could a grownup imagine that they always shared their lunch fairly with their pets? Their innocence was patent, but for days they went about feeling like murderers. It was wiser, better for all concerned, for them to stick to simple jobs, such as trampling the corn or aging their brother's whiskey.

X

Visit of Politeness

IT WAS PURE CHANCE that brought Carmen and Pepita to the road in front of La Tulisa's place. They did have some curiosity about the blind woman's establishment, but even so, they never would have gone to it, certainly would not have stepped inside the gate, by plan. They were sure that the place was filthy, and though the old woman herself fascinated them, she also made them uneasy, as I have told.

When they started drifting along the road they had no plan or destination at all. They moved toward Rociada village because they had turned to the left when they stepped off the grass in front of their house, and they followed the road because they were at loose ends. Being accustomed to finding ample occupation at all times, the condition of being at loose ends bothered them even more than it does most children.

There had been gobbets of rain a few times during the morning; it had not properly cleared until lunchtime. In the night there had been the downpour of a regular mountain thunderstorm, with the lightning flashing almost continuously and constant booming in the heavens. Their father being away, they had run into their mother's room, lit candles, and prayed with her in front of the altar. As a result, they were a trifle short of sleep. They were not out of sorts, but they were jumpy.

Pino had driven their mother and Consuelo into Las Vegas that morning. Consuelo had gone to get her teeth looked over, which was no privilege, but they wished they had been taken along. Las Vegas was a city, the home of assorted aunts and cousins on both the Baca and the Pendaries side, a place where there was always something to see and take home in the mind to think over. Consuelo's going left a slight gap, not only because they were used to being three together, but because she was the middle one. With Carmen eleven, going on twelve, and Pepita seven, the flow between them was not quite as smooth as when the third sister was there to strike an average. Carmen was beginning to have ideas about being grown up and acting like a lady; occasionally she found undiluted Pepita childish. The youngest sister sometimes thought the oldest one was in danger of becoming stuffy.

Rain had left the day cool, too cool for playing in the icehouse. After a morning indoors, they just had to get out of their own four walls. They cast about for occupations. Canuto, of whom they never tired and who, miraculously, never tired of them, was away on his vacation. Their burros had been turned out to pasture. They tried to get Señor Juan to round them up for them, but he had been too busy. Whatever he had been busy with did not make interesting watching, and his mood had been unsociable. The children, knowing that he occasionally went on quite large benders, suspected that he was suffering from what in Spanish is aptly called *violín*. The other two Juans, Juan Grande and Juan Chico, who often furnished entertainment, had gone to help move the beef herd. Right after lunch the maids left for the village on some occasion about which they had not bothered to tell the children. It was just one of those days when, in a purely negative way, things go wrong.

The road had become dry enough in most parts for the dirt to scuff up into reddish-brown dust when they kicked it, but the ruts and chuckholes were muddy, and here and there were puddles, little bodies of water looking like off-color chocolate until you reached the angle at which they mirrored the sky's strong blue. The meadows on either side were wet; they knew that the oak brush and pine woods on the hillsides would be soaking. They felt circumscribed.

They wandered in the direction of the village without any goal at all. Pepita found and caught a small green frog in a wet place in the grassy ditch. She was enchanted with it and wanted to keep it to take home, but Carmen talked her into turning it loose. They noted that the mariposa lilies and wild flags were all gone and the cardinal flowers just beginning to come out. They kept a watch for tiger lilies.

For a time it came upon them to sing as they went along. They sang clearly and accurately "Sur le Pont d'Avignon" several times over. Carmen was the man who bowed at "*Les beaux messieurs font comme ça,*" and Pepita curtsied deeply at the ladies' line. Then they sang "Adelita." They found romance in the love of that fine Mexican warrior, that wild Villista, for his Adelita, and in his determination to follow her by land or by sea if she should go off with anyone else. They sang those lines with special emphasis: " . . . *Por mar en un buque de guerra, Por tierra en un tren militar.*"

Carmen imagined the man, in a straw sombrero, with his rifle in his hand and a bandolier over his shoulder. Then, as she sang, she was bothered by the idea of pursuing someone in a train, even *un tren militar.* A train was a splendid monster with a huge, puffing engine, or even two engines for the pull between Las Vegas and Ratón, as she had seen when she went to the station in town, but it could move only along the line of its rails. She saw herself as the beloved of a soldier, but the soldier had become rather simple, *payaso,* as they said that Mexicans sometimes were. She felt affectionately sorry for him. Now another man came to her window, somewhat resembling Pascual Orozco, who was at once romantic and rather frightening. This man had Pascual's fine profile and keen eyes, but his mustaches were even more sweeping and he was much younger. He would wear a wide black felt sombrero with gold stitching, and charro clothes such as horsemen of good family wore in Mexico. He would take her from her window, she wearing a long flowing skirt and a wide hat with a fluffy feather in it, and carry her off behind him on his big black horse. He would carry her by secret, scrambling trails deep into the Sangre de Cristo Mountains, even beyond Rociada, to the mysterious, hidden places where the whiskey stills were — only somehow this was all across the border in the unknown adventure-teeming land of Mexico and not in the United States, where exciting things stopped happening long ago. As her imagination built its story, she felt definitely sorry for her original, simple lover, scouring the low country on a train. She imagined him sitting astride the engine, scouting to the right and left, his hand above his eyes, and she felt like giggling.

The man would be rather like Pascual, she thought, but nicer as well as younger. There was something wrong about Pascual, a quality that chilled her. That aspect of him was related to something that had happened once when Pino was with him and he killed a dog. She had heard only a vague mention of the incident, and when she asked about it, both Pino and Canuto had refused to tell her, Pino sharply, Canuto with an evasion. The uneasy feeling he gave her, despite her admiration of him, related to that, although it derived from something in the man himself which she could not analyze.

Idling along, within an hour after leaving the house the girls had covered the two miles to the edge of Rociada. The village consisted of a compact arrangement of earth-colored houses, most of them flat-roofed, around a plaza, encircled by an irregular, disjointed ring which included the dance hall. Outside of that, other, more scattered houses reached along the three roads leading from the village.

They were not supposed to visit there unaccompanied.

This was not for fear of any harm that could come to them, but a matter of propriety and probably as well to control children who, once interest had risen above the low threshold of self-consciousness, might get into anything. They stopped by the eastern edge, where the road that goes south to Daily Canyon joins the road from the ranch, contemplating the dullness of simply turning around and going back.

A cottontail ran out on the Daily Canyon road, stood frozen in a rut, and then disappeared, appropriately, into a clump of rabbit brush. They moved after it quietly, not expecting or wishing to catch or harm it, but in the purest instinct of the chase. Here there had been less rain than at the ranch, the bare earth was dusty. They slipped along the opposite side of the road. Pepita stopped just short of the clump, Carmen went by it, then both tiptoed up to it. Delightfully, the rabbit was there, crouching, and they had a chance to see its whiskers and the slight heaving of its sides before it broke and was off into the field beyond.

Brightened by this adventure, they walked on, and thus they came to the fence in front of La Tulisa's place. Whoever had built the fence for her had done a good job, at some long past time. The top of each picket had been cut in the shape of a broad arrowhead, with a semicircle taken out of each side just below to form the neck. The supporting posts were fairly close together, and the horizontal rail was heavy. Since the day the fence was built, however, whenever that was, no nail had been replaced, no piece of wood repaired or straightened if it went askew.

The children had ridden by here often enough, going to or coming from Daily Canyon, where they liked to picnic, but they had never been by there before on foot. They stopped to take a good look.

The house was box-shaped, of adobe, which, having been dug from the soil of the place itself, repeated the reddish color of the bare ground. There was a door in the middle of the front wall, with a rather small, high window on either side of it. The one to the left had been boarded up. Out of the flat roof and the fire wall grew coarse grass and weeds. The fire wall needed recapping; the plaster on the walls was seamed and cracked and in spots had washed entirely away, exposing the adobe bricks underneath. The place looked deserted, but smoke rose from its chimney.

Behind and to one side of the house were an assortment of patched-together sheds and shacks and the relics of a chicken run, its wire gone in places, in places fallen to the ground, curled and entangled with itself. Bits of tumbleweed and dry stalks trapped in the network of the wire provided it with a dead brown fuzz. The yard was bare earth and trash. The trash was sparse, as though there never had been much to throw out of this house, but some of it looked as if it had been there forever. There was a tin can rusted into brown lace, and a piece of heavy white material with eyelets in it that had merged into the earth and turned into a pallid, half-buried skeleton. There was no indication that flowers had ever been planted in the yard, there was not even a single hollyhock. Some chickens moved in the brush behind the house.

Carmen remembered hearing that after Teófila, La Tulisa's daughter, went away three years ago, the blind woman had moved her chickens into the house for convenience. But the chicken run must have been a wreck long before that, she thought, trying to remember if she had noticed when she rode past.

For all the trash and the broken and rotting sheds, the area around the house had qualities of bareness and a sort of cleanliness, rain-washed, snow-scrubbed, windswept, sand-scoured, and sun-beaten. None of these suited its owner. The house, inscrutable, suggestive of darkness within, with heaven knew what contents, was more in keeping with their concept of her.

On a dull day, they both were of a single mind to draw from the sight of the yard and house as much nourishment as they could. They stared and imagined, contemplating the old woman's legend. They had about exhausted the possibilities when Toribio came around the corner of the house. Apart from some dirt on his knees and a smooch on his face he was clean as usual, a healthy infant not quite five. He carried a popgun, which he fired as he came into the yard. Seeing them he called, "*Tengo rifle! Veanse mi rifle!*"

The girls intensely enjoyed playing with younger children, whom they regarded as living dolls, far more fun than any toys. The sight of Toribio created a real temptation.

"Let's go in and talk to him," Pepita said, and then, in Spanish, "Whence didst thou bring the rifle, Toribio?"

"Amadeo gave it to me." He broke it competently,

snapping the breech shut again, and dropped something into the barrel, leaving the cork to dangle on the string. "It shoots really. I have bullets." He aimed at the house and fired. There was a sound of something hitting the wall.

"What class of bullets?" Pepita asked.

"Mere bullets." He spoke in a deepened, boasting voice.

Pepita said, "Let's go see."

Carmen hesitated. "Mamma doesn't want us to go into her house."

"We'll just go in the yard."

"All right."

They went in. Almost immediately the blind woman came to her door, peering out, turning her face widely from side to side as though she looked with her ears. The effect was birdlike and grotesque. "Who is it?"

Pepita had gone directly to the boy. Carmen turned. As her parent's child, she felt an obligation, the more so since La Tulisa was such a wretched object. She moved toward her hesitantly, giving the correct greeting and telling who she was.

The old woman beamed. She responded with the usual invitation to pass within, which, when Carmen refused it, she repeated with real meaning. Carmen felt caught. She had been deeply imbued with the idea that one must respect the sensibilities of the poor. In the face of insistence, not to step inside for a moment would be rude. Reluctantly she did so, praying that she would not be offered food, and reluctantly she lowered herself into a wooden chair, sitting bolt upright because there were chicken-droppings on the crosspiece at the back.

The room had a bed in one corner. At the head of the bed was a pillow covered with some threadbare, grayly dirty material, at the other end several heavy quilts piled without folding. In the middle, on the bare, hard, stained mattress, a hen rested serenely. Over the iron headpiece hung a towel on which could be seen all the dirt that had been removed from Toribio in the past week. There was a table with an oilcloth cover from which much of the surface was gone, and on that some unwashed dishes. In the corner opposite the bed stood the stove, with an old lard pail, a coffeepot, and a frying pan on top of it. The black dog, lying in front of it, looked at her briefly, wagged its tail, and went back to sleep. Items of clothing were here and there about the room and on nails in the walls; a hopelessly fly-specked chromo of the Sacred Heart hung over the bed. There were some rickety shelves carrying items of food, a rusty washtub on the floor, a number of old boxes and equally old shoes, a water bucket with a dipper.

On one of the boxes stood a granite-ware, enamel wash-basin and beside it a plate containing two speckled eggs — to one of which a downy feather adhered — a vigil lamp, a small piece of yellow soap, a comb, and several safety pins. There was logic in this assemblage in a blind woman's house, as they were objects pertaining to the grandchild's care.

The two windows, the smallish one beside the door and the larger one, facing west, in the back wall, were nearly opaque. Their lower halves were further obscured by glass curtains, probably originally white, now streaked, darker and lighter, according to the ridges and valleys of their folds. Along the lines of some of these folds were rents, not tears but failures of the material from the weight and caustic of age and filth. On the ledge of the back window were three cans of different sizes in which dirt still remained, and in one some dead stumps of the flowers someone had once raised there.

A doorway without a door gave on the second room, which for all its boarded-up window was lighter than the one in which Carmen sat. She guessed at an open door facing west. From her chair, she could see only a small slice of it, but enough to tell that that was where the chickens lived. It was quite apparent that they made themselves free of the living room as well.

Even with the door open, the room she was in was dark. It had the quality of darkness. The once whitewashed walls were stained and blotched to the point of suggesting formless, unpleasant pictures. The dark, smoke-coated wooden ceiling, the angles of its meeting with the walls, and the four corners were richly draped with cobwebs. La Tulisa's three black shawls hung on one wall with a suggestion of personalities of their own. Carmen knew that, manners or no manners, she would be out of there quickly.

The old woman, not even feeling her way, sat down on the other chair, and asked politely after Carmen's mamma and papa. Carmen answered. Then the dog growled faintly. La Tulisa stiffened. The doorway was darkened by the big form of Pascual Orozco in his wide black hat and his dark suit. He took off his hat and greeted the old woman, who replied to his formal courtesies in a neutral voice. Her manner had changed, she seemed uneasy. Then Pascual looked at Carmen, raised an eyebrow to indicate surprise at seeing her there, and wished her good afternoon. He managed somehow, with the look and the commonplace words, to make her feel childish and unimportant. He, too, went through the form of asking after her family, but it was mere form.

Pascual squatted in the doorway. As he made himself comfortable he looked at the blind woman with a smile which lacked kindness; he had the air of a hard man who had come to obtain an end. Suddenly Carmen was thinking of that vague tale of the killing of the dog, and she remembered the feeling of emphasis she had received from Pino's and Canuto's refusals to speak of it. She wanted to leave, but she did not think Pascual would rise and stand aside for her, and she knew she could not brush past him. Nor could she, being whose child she was, simply retreat through the other room and out the chickens' doorway.

Pascual said to La Tulisa, "And what with thee, old woman?"

"Halfway well for a poor blind woman, but I think about my grandchild. For a long time now thou hast given me nothing for the little one."

There was a faint whine in her voice. Carmen, listening, was surprised that she should expect Pascual to do anything for the child.

"There'll be something for him, perhaps." Pascual

paused. Outside the house Carmen heard Toribio's gun go *pop!* and then the sound of a light missile striking the wall, followed by her sister's cheerful voice. She wished she were out there. Pascual went on talking to La Tulisa, ignoring the girl and following the irritating practice of grownups who think that if they discuss their business with oblique references a listening child cannot understand.

"Today in the night I bring supplies from more above. I want to leave them in thy sheds until I can take them out the Sunday."

Carmen knew perfectly well what he meant by supplies. He was certainly not talking about stolen horses.

The blind woman said, "That no. Thou hast plenty of places in where to hide them."

Pascual said, "The Federals have been riding around my canyons. They found one of my places, and now they are searching everywhere up there. Thus, for a little I must hide them differently. Until they go away, thy sheds are the best."

"No. I have fear. Very well thou knowest they have been in the village, too."

"Thou hast fear? Fear of what, old woman?" Pascual sounded mocking.

"That they will seize me, that they will put me prison, as they did Juanico."

"That thou sayest to them that thou art blind, that thou knowest nothing of it. Besides, they will not come looking."

Carmen could not help listening, watching, and thinking intently. The various processes of bootlegging were taken calmly in that section, and no one lacked for whiskey and wine of sorts, but there was a big difference between buying the stuff and being in the business. It did not matter what the actual danger might be; what mattered to her so that she almost brought herself to intervene was that this poor old creature was terrified. There were federal agents in the mountains at that time, and Carmen was old enough and sensitive enough to imagine what horrific visions of arrest and prison La Tulisa saw within her darkness. To mix her into bootlegging at all was unthinkable. Outside, the gun kept on popping and Pepita and Toribio chattered together.

"I saw Teófila in Las Vegas," Pascual said casually, as though he had dropped the former subject.

"The poor little thing! Is she better? How is she? That thou owest to God to help her."

"She is out of the hospital, but she has no strength. She still must keep going to the doctor. She needs a little more time without working. That takes money."

La Tulisa said, "Money."

"It may be that I can take care of it. Otherwise, if she commences to work now, I fear that it might finish her. It pleases me to take care of my friends, of my friends' children. Good friends are those who help one."

"Hast thou no heart?"

Pascual laughed, and Carmen hated him completely. "For those who have heart for me." He stood up. "There is thy grandchild to take care of, and thy daughter who has great necessity." He studied the old woman's face.

"Thou art not going to hear anything if someone comes by thy sheds tonight?"

La Tulisa said in a low voice, "I shall not hear anything." She was twisting her hands together and a pair of tears shone on her cheeks. Almost inaudibly she said, "I have fear," but Pascual had left the doorway.

Carmen sat quite still for about a minute, fighting away the understanding of fear and cruelty. La Tulisa had dug her beads out from somewhere among her rags and was praying. Silently, Carmen left the room.

Outside, Pepita and Toribio squatted on the ground. They had been watching Pascual swing to his saddle and now, as he rode off, their heads turned back, facing the house. Pepita's expression was one of delightful absorption. Toribio said, "Thy turn," and handed her the gun. She cocked it, slipped something in the muzzle, raised it, and fired. The *pop!* was followed by a distinct *splat!* against the adobe. Carmen saw that part of the wall in front of the children was dotted with dark marks.

"What on earth are you shooting?" she asked in English.

"*Serrotes,* look, they're nice and dry." Pepita held out her left hand, with three dry, hard sheep turds in it.

Something let loose inside Carmen. "Of all the nasty things! You put those down right away!"

Pepita's face set, her lower lip thrust itself out. Carmen knew the look, and the stubbornness that went with it. At that moment she could not have stood an argument. She wanted to be in her own home as soon as possible. More calmly she said, "It's late. We'd better get on home. Mamma wouldn't like it if she knew we'd been here, so we'd better get there before she comes back or she'll be asking us where we've been."

Reluctantly her sister dropped the ammunition and got to her feet. She handed the popgun back to Toribio with thanks. He was sorry to see her go.

"Come along," Carmen insisted, "it's late."

"It's not so late."

On the road, Pepita said, "What's your hurry?" And then, "What did Pascual want in there? You were certainly in there a long time."

"He didn't want anything, he was just talking. *Serrotes* — of all the dirty things — " All the reactions pent within her exploded and Carmen poured forth anger. Pepita was astonished, then she responded with her own temper. They fought bitterly all the way home and carried the fight on inside the house until Doña Marguerite, back from Las Vegas, stopped them abruptly. Carmen afterwards could never say what had made her so angry.

XI

The Cap in the Snow

MOUNTAIN COUNTRY, like the seacoast, is enemy to incredulity. The very name of Consuelo's range of mountains, Sierra de la Sangre de Cristo, has the ring of wonders. The first Spaniards felt their hearts uplifted when, after months of antlike marching across the baking southern deserts, they came upon these snow-capped peaks. And when, at sunset, they saw the shining whiteness all across the eastern horizon turn to a glow of carmine tinged with purple, the sense of awe and beauty filled them. With faith and poetry they gave the range its name, Mountains of the Blood of Christ — surely one of the strongest in all geography.

Behind that western rampart, the Sangre de Cristos are not just the seen chain of mountains but a broad region of highlands. This region is both peaceful and violent. It consists of fertile watered valleys guarded by rugged, masculine, protective hills, and of higher sky-challenging peaks beyond. It consists of mountain meadows laced by trout streams and brilliant with flowers, and of endless dark forests. It is a land of wild turkey, deer, and elk, and of bear, coyote, mountain lion, and the ever possible, most certainly to be believed in, surviving, murderous timber wolf. It is a land sleeping under day after day of quiet, unsullied sunshine, and a land of sudden intemperate winds and storms of every sort.

The people, for the most part Spanish with varying proportions of Indian blood, are like the country. They are friendly, courteous, hospitable, simple, and charged with latent danger. At wedding feasts and other such celebrations, it is common enough for fights to break out and weapons to be drawn. These disputes do not ordinarily result in a killing, and unless they do the police are kept out of the matter. While I would not say that Consuelo (and her sisters) grew up accustomed to sudden death, by the time she was ten news of a stabbing or a shooting at Casimiro's dance hall would call forth lively comment but would neither surprise nor shock.

The mountain people brought with them and preserved the lore of seventeenth-century Spain. To this was added a seasoning from other equally ancient cultures — the tales and mysteries that a Tewa, Apache, Navajo, or Comanche captive wife might whisper to her children by firelight. There were few who doubted that the Sangre de Cristos were populated by far more than the eye was ordinarily permitted to see.

Such families as Baca y Pendaries, educated, traveled, *gente de razón,* of course took no stock in the superstitions of the ignorant, except for certain portents concerning the weather. When Consuelo's parents recounted any of the tales, they did so with amusement, scouting them in the telling. Miss Eufemia was not interested in the myths and superstitions of people who in her own country before it was ruined by the revolutions would have been peons. She held that her pupils, simply as a matter of their birth, should be immune to their inferiors' credulities.

Consuelo, at ten years of age, or Carmen, or Pepita, if asked, would unhesitatingly have denied belief in magic and ghosts, and in so doing would have been quite sincere. Yet back of unbelief there was the sense of a possibility, half consciously reserved — a rather creepy, magical enrichment of their world.

They had always the feeling that in those mountains anything could happen. There was, for instance, the experience Pino had when he was home from college for the Christmas vacation. For some reason now forgotten — some matter of repairs or painting — he slept in a vacant room off the living room for the first few nights. The front door opened directly into the living room, opposite the big stone fireplace. Unfailingly it was locked at night, yet on the second night of Pino's vacation, in the dark, cold time before there was even a hint of dawn, he woke to hear heavy footsteps in the living room. Then he heard a thud and a grunt, as of a man running into an unseen chair.

He swung out of bed and reached for a weapon. Not being in his own room, he could not lay his hand on a gun, but his chilly foot touched one of his boots. He picked that up and crept, shivering, to the door, which he opened as silently as he could. It was completely dark beyond; the last spark of the fire was long dead. He thought that he could make out a dim area of lightness where the front door should be; otherwise he could see nothing, but he was sure of a stranger's presence. He listened, heard breathing, then a step. He hurled the boot in the direction of the sound, swearing and yelling at the intruder, in Spanish, to get out.

The boot struck something with a faint whack, and this was followed by a sharper sound as the boot dropped to the floor. There was another grunt, then heavy footsteps going to the front door — the steps of a drunk, Pino thought, peculiar in rhythm and with a drag to them. Part of the lighter area there was momentarily blocked. He slammed the door, locked it, and returned to his bed in a hurry. It was not until the next morning, when they all could see the muddy tracks on the polished floor and the imprints in the snow outside, that he learned he had flung his boot at a large bear.

The incident was rich enough in itself to satisfy the older Bacas, but the three little girls, still of an age to converse at length with servants, soon learned that there was more to it than their parents realized. To say simply that a bear had come into the house left too much to be explained. What was an ordinary bear doing roaming about when it should be hibernating? How could a mere bear open a locked door? Or, even assuming that the door had by some strange accident been left unlocked on this sole occasion, how would an animal know how to turn the knob? It was out of the question that the door could have been left ajar in winter weather; the cold air rushing in would immediately have caught the attention of whoever was last in the room. And, more, if you hit a bear, the bear would surely attack you — not flee, as this creature had done. Pino had said, among other things, "*Por Dios,*" invoking the name of God; that was what had routed the visitor. There was a smell of *brujería* — of witchcraft — in the air.

Seña Delfina, who did the Bacas' fine laundry, was the little girls' ultimate authority on supernatural matters that lay beyond the purview of the church; she was a person one would expect to be familiar with the strange and magical. There was a mystery about her origin, to begin with. She came from over beyond Mora, toward the Colorado border. The place was never exactly identified, just as her maiden name somehow remained unknown. She spoke better Spanish than the other villagers, with a less slurred pronunciation. She looked Castilian — a tall, straight-backed, angular old woman, with a clear skin, an aquiline nose, and hazel eyes. She was always impressive, with a black fringed shawl covering her shoulders, and a full, bell-shaped Spanish-style skirt under which her many petticoats rustled.

The girls duly sought Seña Delfina's opinion about the bear when they paid her a pre-Christmas visit. The excuse for the visit was to bring her a quantity of playing cards from a used-up deck — a gift she prized, because the ashes of three cards, of any suit or number, burned in the proper manner and placed on the forehead, throat, and chest, were the best of all remedies for colds.

Seña Delfina was married to Emeterio Pineda, who was

said to be her third husband. Consuelo thought of Señor Emeterio as a gingerbread man. He was small, broad, and brown, with a blobby brown nose and black, round raisin eyes. They lived in a house that belonged deep in a forest, for children to come upon by accident. From the outside it was just one more red-brown cube of adobe, except for the window lintels. There were two windows facing the road, set rather high on each side of the door. Ordinarily, in adobe construction a long beam is set in the wall over any aperture, extending well beyond it on both sides, to distribute the load of earth and roof above. Whoever built Seña Delfina's house had had the fantasy of using, instead, the two halves of a curved ox yoke. Painted blue to match the trim, they arched above the windows. It was inescapable that the house was the upper part of a cheerfully surprised face, with the door for a nose, and the children were sure that if one could ever see the mouth, it would be smiling.

The combined kitchen and living room, into which one entered, was sparsely furnished and very clean. The walls were painted to shoulder height with a dado of *tierra amarilla,* a natural, fine, yellow-buff pigment sparkling with powdered mica. Across the far end ran a row of high, small, square windows — so high that Consuelo could see only the orchard tree-tops and the sky when she looked through them. In each window was a potted plant, neatly tended. The effect was of a series of still-lifes in deep frames. At floor level in the middle of the same wall, a neat miniature arch had been cut through to allow the cats to go in and out.

Seña Delfina did the Bacas' fine laundry as much because she had a passion for laundering as for the money. When they engaged in special entertaining, she usually came to help out. Many of their guests lived in the mountain region or had visited Don José's often enough to be acquainted with Rociada, and knew the old woman. Sometimes she was invited into the living room after dinner and offered a glass of whiskey, which she relished. (She also liked to drink good strong *chile* neat, from a cup.) After she had taken the liquor, if anyone would play, she would dance. It was a curious, stiff-legged wooden-soldier sort of dance, with gliding steps from the waltz, occasional hops derived from the polka and the schottische (known in New Mexico as the *xardís*), and sometimes the stamping movement of *el chinche* (the Bedbug) — so called because you stamp as if trying to kill one. She danced gravely, with her head high and her arms by her sides. I have seen both Consuelo and Pepita, as grown women, dance in this manner on occasion, apparently quite unconscious of imitating a childhood impression.

Once in a great while Seña Delfina stayed the night in the Bacas' house. When that happened, the three girls waited until they heard her go to her room; then they scurried to it, to sit for an hour on her bed and listen to her stories of *brujos* and *brujas* — the male and female witches who turn themselves into animals or balls of fire or winds when they go forth to work their evil. The little girls had heard of these creatures often enough, but Seña Delfina was equipped with a satisfying plenty of detail and known instances. She also knew about the little bearded men who inhabit the high mountains and appear only in order to bedevil woodcutters and shepherds, and she could recite exactly what they had said to Benigno Reyes after they had caused him to get lost. Seña Delfina did not make a point of discussing magic with the girls, but she responded readily and fully when they asked about it. As to the bear, she would not flatly commit herself, but she was certain that it had been more than just an ordinary bear.

One reserved a little place of belief, no matter what the grown-up members of the family might say. It was, rather, half belief, held to because to lose it would take some of the excitement out of the world. Deeper than that, Consuelo, at least, had a feeling that she had never stopped to define; her mountains as a whole had a personality with many aspects, not all of which were bright or kind. Such things as *brujería* might be a manifestation of the dark aspects, or they might be no more than the fancies of people, having no relation to that other, unarguable presence.

The year of the bear was particularly rich in supernatural manifestations. In the late summer, Epifanio Gutiérrez was unable to cross the Río Manuelitas to get home because of a *bruja* who manifested herself as a number of balls of fire. Epifanio finally gave up, turned back, and spent the night with friends on the road to Peñasco. Not long after that Carmen, Consuelo, and Pepita were playing at the edge of the river, about half a mile below where Epifanio met the *bruja,* between their father's house and the lower ranch. A shadow fell on them, and all three turned to see who might be standing on the high ground, but there was no one. The shadow had lasted only a moment, but each of them had noticed it independently, and even before they went through the motions of searching for a possible prankster in hiding, they were afraid. They came home early, and for several days watched for some occurence, such as a sudden death or a fire, to justify a portent.

Snow was on the ground when Policarpio Lobato was bothered one day by a fox that skulked with unusual daring around his outbuildings and chicken run. Near sundown, when he went to get firewood, the animal just stood and looked at him from a slight distance. He had a strange feeling that he knew the creature, and that it knew him by name and was mocking him. He signed himself, and then threw a billet of stove wood at it, striking it on the left shoulder hard enough to knock it over. It ran off limping. Within a day, everyone had heard that an old man who lived in Ratón Canyon, and about whom there was a good deal of suspicion, had been laid up with a sudden violent attack of arthritis in the left shoulder. No one could ask for clearer evidence of *brujería.*

As I have said, Pino's encounter with the bear came just before Christmas. Early in January, Dionisia, the miller's wife, who was a strange, moody woman and a magnificent pastry cook, came running across the meadow shortly after dark and threw herself into the Bacas' kitchen. She was so terrified that it was some time before she could speak. She had come up from the mill, which was on the lower ranch, and at about where the shadow had fallen upon the girls, the same fiery *bruja* Epifanio saw had taken out after her. Doña Marguerite finally had to have Juan Grande routed out of the bunkhouse to see her home.

Most people when they grow up largely lose contact with the reality of their childhood, substituting for it the clichés and stereotypes of their time and culture. Events they can recite fairly accurately, but the content has been drained from them. Now and again, one encounters somebody who has retained much of that early reality — who, in the act of remembering, can recover not only events but also thoughts and attitudes. What you are presented with by such a person is the living experience, intangible, often unwordable, intensely subjective. My wife has this kind of memory.

The wishful half belief in little men, *brujería,* and magic is, of course, long gone. What remains came out one night when we had driven home through snow from a dinner party and, as we warmed ourselves at the fire, she began to tell about Pepita's cap. Her telling of it was simple. Much of the story I am going to try to set down was in her face and voice.

A week or so after Dionisia was chased by the *bruja,* the girls rode down to the lower ranch. The place had been built by their Grandfather Pendaries, and was at this time occupied by cousins, except for quarters set aside for Dionisia and Nicanor, the miller. A soft snowfall had ended before noon, and the afternoon was all porcelain and gold. The girls had spent the whole morning in the school room with Miss Eufemia, and well over another hour there after dinner. Out of conscience, their governess had insisted on a struggle with arithmetic, fully as exasperating to her as to them, until the three little girls were ready to explode. Turned loose at last, they sang and chattered as they rode, and passing the spot where Dionisia had first seen the *bruja,* joked about it, as superior and immune as their parents. They spent some time visiting with their cousins. Then, although the sun was close to setting, they went around by the mill, which at this season of the year was closed down.

A heavy chill was beginning to take the sparkle from the air as they started on the two-mile ride home. That was not enough to lower their spirits; rather, in resistance to the rapid aging of the day, their gaiety became wilder, as though a frenzy had seized them. Carmen invented one of her frequent dramas, assigning parts to each of them. This led to greater silliness, exaggerated acting, and teasing. By pure chance, Consuelo's part set her in opposition to the other two. When Carmen and Pepita suddenly whipped up their horses and galloped on ahead, Consuelo, sticking to a role, and also offended, continued at a trot.

The other two disappeared into the woods through which the trail led. By the time Consuelo reached the edge of the woods, the mountains to westward hid the sun. She rode under the trees, feeling hurt and lonely. The woods were completely silent. With the light going and the snow turning blue, they seemed strange. The trees made snow arches over her head, each limb carrying its fluffy cover. She was conscious of a beauty that almost hurt, and at the same time she felt out of reach of all mankind, deserted, and angry at being deserted, and afraid of she did not quite know what.

Beyond the woods waited the meadow, with the river, black between snow-piled banks, alongside. That was where the shadow had fallen upon them, and the *bruja* had chased Dionisia. These incidents did not seem funny now. At this hour, in her aloneness and the swing from her high mood, her home country was the land of dark forests and harsh peaks, of bears and wolves, of knife fights and barn burnings, of little men, ghosts, and the evil-working, secret community of *brujería.* Stubbornness made her hold the white horse, Concho, to an easy trot. She would not give in to vague fears, nor would she give the two who had so meanly deserted her the satisfaction of having her come racing to catch up with them. Concho was safe and old, but he wanted to get to shelter and feed; he fretted at the bit, danced a little, and pricked up and turned his ears, and when a branchload of snow slipped to the ground with a faint *whoosh,* he shied. In the reasoning part of her mind, Consuelo knew why the horse acted as he did, but another part suggested that he, too, found reason for alarm in the solitude, and his very dependability made this the more significant. Often the tales told how a dog or a horse detected the presence that Christians could not see or hear.

On her left, toward the west, there was a small natural clearing. As she rode into it, a shaft of ruddy gold still reached along the snow, fading away as she came to it, as though it were being pulled back. Not quite in the shaft of light lay a piece of vermilion material with a tassel at one end. Consuelo looked at it twice before she recognized it as Pepita's stocking cap. As soon as the direct light was gone, the cap began to darken, discolored by the blueness that spread over all the ground.

Up to that point, the trail had been marked only by the tracks of the two horses who had gone ahead in single file — a narrow sequence of hoofprints with the dragged lines in between where the hoofs swung forward without clearing the snow. Beside where the cap lay, the snow had been trampled. Consuelo saw that one or both horses had shied really badly — violently enough to dislodge a knitted cap. She drew rein instinctively, and, probably in response to his rider's uneasiness, Concho moved sidewise, his ears sharply forward, blowing slightly through his nostrils.

Suddenly the cap, its brightness gone, lying there empty, became charged with meaning and terror. From the cap the pure quality of fear extended to the sign of frightened horses, to the silent surrounding area, and to the overhanging, white-limbed trees, but the dreadfulness was concentrated in the abandoned article, forlorn on the snow. Staring at it, Consuelo was aware of no specific thing — only the certainty of menace and a will to strike. She slackened the reins and swung their long, Western-style ends against the horse's rump. He went forward at a lope, then broke from the lope into a dead run.

They left the woods and crossed the meadow. She did not think of Dionisia or the shadow, or bears or *brujería;*

she wanted only, with tormented earnestness, to be home and inside four walls. Not until they were almost there and the yellow-lighted windows were clear before her did she remember discipline and pull her horse up, to bring him in with a semblance of proper care.

Her pleasure in the lore that such people as Seña Delfina dealt in did not, of course, end forthwith. It was at this time, however, that the sense of a greater perceived reality first lessened that pleasure through a feeling that those beliefs were lesser and rather childish.

XII

The Wind from the Sea

WHEN CONSUELO was getting on toward fourteen, a change took place in her attitude toward the Rociada country. All through her childhood that country had seemed to her as secure and eternal as the mountains that surrounded it; now, when she came home from the convent school in Santa Fe for a weekend or for the longer holidays, she found it necessary to reassure herself that the long, wide, fertile valley, the three villages, the big ranch, and the mountains were indeed unchanged.

The fact is that mountains are not eternal. Rains and rivers, the pale children of the sea, erode them. It is the uniform gray sea that will last as long as the earth lasts, and the sea is forever recapturing the land, first seeping in and then engulfing. The ancient water is forever wearing the young peaks down to the level of its own monotony. There is a like process constantly at work in the affairs of men.

To the Bacas, Rociada was much more than a place; it was a manner of life containing highly individual elements and rich with the retention of old good things. The Bacas of my generation all grew up serenely sure that the material and nonmaterial aspects of Rociada were firmly established for the ages.

When they were children, ranch, villages, valley, mountains, forests, people, and animals supplied them with a complete and sufficient world. Visits to the city of Las Vegas might be fun, but they were in the nature of amiable sorties from a fastness to which one would unfailingly return. The requirements of education took them, one by one, to schools away from home, but these absences were no more than interruptions. However much one might enjoy seeing something of the outer world, however interesting, or even exciting, one might find it, to Rociada one returned. Around Rociada they all would build their lives.

The first shaking of certainty occurred when their father died. Don José had seemed to them to dominate the landscape as he did the community. He had been getting ready to run for governor of New Mexico, and the odds favored both his nomination and his election; then suddenly he was sick, and then suddenly he was dead. It was as if a piece had fallen out of the sun. It is significant, I think, that all the talk of the old times I have heard from Doña Marguerite and from the others has included little more about Don José's death than that it happened. Talk of the years before is full of him; tales of what happened later are dated as after his passing. It is a dividing point of history, but the event itself is not for reminiscence.

Still, the sun kept on rising whole and round. The mountains stood unchanged. Pino took over the management of the ranch in collaboration with his mother. The three youngest children could adjust themselves to the idea — astonishing, and yet, when everything was considered, reasonable — that even without their father Rociada continued.

If in the recital of the next events there is a sound of *post hoc, propter hoc,* that is not far from the way Consuelo saw it when she was entering her teens. Strange sad things began happening in the outside world, in such purely fabulous places as Wall Street and Australia. According to the evening talk of older people, a sort of disease of poverty had struck even the most distant nations, and in the United States there was the depression. More specifically, the bottom dropped out of the price of wool on the Boston market at the time of the spring shearing. It was not quite clear to Consuelo why the low price of wool in Boston should affect them so directly in New Mexico, but it did. She gathered, further, that the price of fall lambs was likely to be just as bad. And listening, she experienced once more the deep uneasiness, as though in spite of the encircling mountains she felt on her cheek a breath of wind from the sea, chill with fog and monotony.

The world's condition did not mend. It grew worse. Pino and Doña Marguerite sat up late consulting and going over books, sometimes with Señor Juan. Señor Juan was not much on books, but he knew most of what there was to know about pasturage, feed, probable losses from natural causes, and the ways of buyers. Consuelo heard talk of debts. There was, then, an element of uncertainty where nothing but perfect certainty had ever existed.

When she came home from school, with her sisters or alone, she was likely to saddle a horse and ride out to see that everything was unchanged, and everything was, as far as she could tell. The forested mountains ringed the green valley, in the meadows of which, in late May, at the beginning of the long vacation, the pale-blue wild irises were scattered. From the ranch she could see the red-brown adobe houses of the village, with the church in the middle of them. She could ride to Upper Rociada, and then to Gascón, and look in the chapel there to see whether the image of San José still had on the red mittens the women knitted for his hands every winter.

The very name Rociada had been bestowed by her grandfather, in preference to an older one he considered unworthy of the beauty he found there. As for Gascón, it was his own creation. The ranch there had passed out of the family when Consuelo was small. That this should have been allowed to happen was a living regret, but the new owner, Lockridge, had won acceptance as a good neighbor. He ran the place as a dude ranch in the summers, and this brought into the valley a number of people who obviously did not belong there but even more whom the older Bacas, at least, enjoyed. The summer visitors had become part of the familiar scene, and the natives of the tiny settlement still formed part of the greater Rociada community.

In spite of what was happening in the outside world, in Rociada lands and houses remained as they had always been, and so did the daily happenings. The settlements and the ranch were interlaced in such a way that beyond Consuelo's own family there extended a sort of neighborhood family, in which all faces were known and friendly, and everyone was placed as exactly as in the household hierarchy of older and younger children. There were the few whom one addressed as Señor or Señora with their last names, the considerable number who were Señor or Seña with their first names, and the majority, whom one called by their first names alone. (The titles of Don and Doña were held only by Bacas and Pendaries.) All these people called the girl simply Consuelo, but when she was a little older they would become more formal.

The interchange of visits and gifts continued as it had always been. One could not enter a house in the village without accepting something to eat, you made it a rule to bring some present with you, and visitors to the ranch were received as ever. Still the successful hunters and fishermen stopped by to present Doña Marguerite with a bit of game or fish — as like as not out of season. There was no change in that, nor in the feeding and lodging of friends, relatives, and passing strangers. The open hand was in no wise stinted.

I have been reciting minutiae, because they were parts of a ritual of life by means of which, as long as it remained intact, Consuelo could exorcise her uneasiness. The ritual of small things and the greater operation of the ranch, both unchanged, reassured her. The beef herd ranged the hillsides at the edge of the valley. The horses not in use ran wild in the horse pasture. That part of the Baca flocks that grazed near home had not diminished, and at the times of the drives, other bands — five hundred or a thousand at a time — came by, seeming to fill the whole of the sky with their bleating. One could know that prices were still dropping, yet the sight of these animals and the knowledge of still other herds, out of sight, seemed to insure prosperity.

In the fall of Consuelo's fourteenth year, Pino began taking out hunting parties. Consuelo, being back in school, saw nothing of them, but the news that he was doing as a business what he had often done for pleasure disturbed her. She could not see how he could bring himself to do such a thing. If strangers turned up at Rociada, as long as they were at all presentable, you took them in. If Pino liked them and they wanted to go hunting, he might seize the chance to take a few days off and show them the good places. That was totally unlike going out and finding wealthy outlanders who paid to be put up, outfitted, and guided. The wind from the sea was on Consuelo's face again; it was cold and forlorn.

She returned to Rociada for the long summer vacation, which from the vantage point of May seemed an inexhaustible treasure of time. A little over a month before, she had turned fourteen. She considered fourteen a grown-up age, and that made it impossible for her to balk when Doña Marguerite told her she must take care of Evelyn Tisdale.

Miss Tisdale, from St. Louis, had turned up early at

Gascón. Lockridge was not yet ready to handle guests; he was remodeling, and would have no wranglers available for a week or more. He could not at that moment devote himself to the care of a lone, complete tenderfoot, yet he did not want to turn her away. She had just arrived in New Mexico, she was full of eagerness, and if she went to one of the dude outfits on the Pecos River, over the main ridge to the west, he would probably lose her for the season. He asked Doña Marguerite to take her over for a week or ten days as a paying guest, and since the Bacas had not yet brought the gentle horses from the pasture (and the gentlest of these would have to be topped off a few times after it came in), he furnished a pair of his dude-broken horses for the guest and whoever should handle her.

Doña Marguerite selected Consuelo to be Miss Tisdale's guide and instructress. The two oldest girls were still at college, Pepita was too young, and Carmen, her mother must have thought, a trifle too high-spirited; so the duty went to Consuelo. Consuelo was not pleased. Her family was not in the dude business. Nothing had been said to suggest that they were going into it. But once again they were selling what they had always given, and she feared that this might be a second step, following the first step of the hunting parties, and that then there would be a third, and so on, until they had walked away entirely from pride and freedom.

On the first morning she studied her charge with mistrust. Miss Tisdale wore a smallish felt hat, a tweed riding jacket, and tight jodhpurs. She was youngish, moderately tall, and more than plump. She had brown hair, a fair skin, and good-enough features; she would have come under the heading of "nice-looking" if it had not been for her eyes, which were too pale a blue. Consuelo definitely objected to the eyes. By and large, she lived among brown-eyed people, but there are plenty of gray- and green-eyed Spanish Americans, and among the Anglo cattlemen and sheepmen of her acquaintance not a few had eyes as light as Miss Tisdale's. All these people, however, had a sort of edge to their gaze. Their eyes were used to having lots of space to work in, able to spot the movement of a deer in a forest, to find the stray sheep or cow on the distant hillside. This young woman had city eyes, amiable, unlooking. As Canuto brought up the horses, a buckskin under Consuelo's saddle, a brown for the guest, Consuelo was pushing away the dreadful idea that from now on her days at home might be taken up with wrangling women like this. She would, she thought, much sooner pack a burro and go herd sheep.

Although Canuto had become completely naturalized to Rociada, he had never forgotten Southern tricks of service. He gave the newcomer a leg up, and Consuelo noted with disgust that Miss Tisdale needed it and that Canuto really lifted. She swung to her own saddle and they started off.

Consuelo hadn't the faintest conception of what it is like not to know how to ride, nor had she any grasp of the many other points dude wranglers must keep in mind. She had planned on one of her own favorite rides, by the road that skirted Rociada village and led over the ridges to the south into Daily Canyon, and thence, in a circuit, down the canyon to the east and back to the ranch. For her alone, it would have made just about a good morning on horseback. This time, she soon saw, things were going to be different.

Miss Tisdale was brave but awkward when her horse walked, in real trouble when it trotted, and terrified when Consuelo got her to try a lope. They crawled along, down the road past the ranch, and then, turning to the left, along the cart track by the outlying houses of the village. The greenhorn began to feel at ease at a walk, and flooded her guide with questions. In a different mood Consuelo would have been highly diverted by the young woman's ignorance and pleased by the respect shown to her, as well as by the romance Miss Tisdale plainly found in the Baca family and its setting. She did not, however, intend to be amused or pleased, any more than she had allowed herself to recognize the admiration in those pale-blue eyes when she first appeared in her faded levis, boots, and tinkling spurs. Also, unfortunately, Miss Tisdale had betrayed the fact that she thought the natives of Rociada were Mexicans, which suggested that she might think the same thing even of the Bacas. Consuelo treated her with a smooth, dire politeness that is profoundly Spanish, the meaning of which was quite lost on the recipient.

It was not just mud, Consuelo told her. It was adobe, which has to be carefully mixed and dried. Yes, even here where timber was so plentiful they preferred to build with adobe, because it gave better insulation. The brand on the buckskin read "H-bar-S"; she did not know what ranch it belonged to. That on the brown was "CS," which meant that it came from an outfit over by Wagon Mound. The Bacas' brand was "Wineglass-2." Well, it was a sort of U, with a bar coming down from it, and a figure 2 hanging from that. No, she did not think that branding was cruel. It hurt for a moment, but that was all. She had seen a calf get to his feet immediately after being branded (she did not mention what else had been done to the calf) and immediately trot to his mother and begin nursing. No, there were no Indians at Rociada; the people were all *Spanish-Americans* except Canuto, who was Anglo. There was a *Mexican* who had settled just outside the village some years ago, but he had wound up in the penitentiary. The nearest Indians were at Taos. That little bunch of cattle over there belonged to Pascual Orozco. Yes, those were wild irises; later in the year there would be tiger lilies. No, she never carried a gun, but Pino usually wore one when he was riding far. And so on and on.

By the time they got to Daily Canyon, a wild, rugged, beautiful place of cliffs and big trees, Consuelo was figuring how to shorten the ride. At a couple of level stretches, she had managed to get Miss Tisdale to stay with an easy fox trot, but it was plain that they could never make the usual circuit. Then she heard thunder and, looking upward, saw fat gleaming clouds high above the western mountains. It was early in the season for thunderstorms, but there was a big one coming up, and Daily Canyon was no place in which to let it catch you. The canyon was a notorious attracter of thunderbolts. In fact, one of its charms, for Consuelo, was the tall riven trees one encountered there. When thunder rolled again, she said they would have to turn back and they had better hurry.

On the back trail, the horses had more will to go, and their willingness was increased by a cool little wind that sprang up, died, and then blew again. They kept breaking from a walk to a fox trot, and then to a true trot. Consuelo did hold her horse down and moderate the pace, but even so she let the animals travel at a gait that made her dude uneasy.

The clouds were nearly overhead, the thunder was loud, and the wind smelled strongly of rain when they came to the place, not far from Rociada village, where the trail branched off to Gascón. Both horses wanted to follow it. Consuelo controlled the buckskin easily enough, but the docile brown was too much for the Easterner. Hauling awkwardly at long reins, she got the horse to circling, but she could not straighten him out. Lightning flashed brilliantly in the west, and loud thunder came hard upon it. The brown horse danced, kicked, and then began to pitch. Consuelo slipped from her saddle, grabbed the animal's bridle, and told her charge to dismount. Miss Tisdale did so as fast as she could, and in the process nearly fell.

Consuelo said, "We'll lead them along the road a little way. Then they'll be all right and we can get back on them. We've got to get to shelter as quick as we can."

They led their horses well past the turnoff. Then Consuelo held the brown horse's bridle near the bit and instructed her charge to take the reins in her left hand and grasp the horn with the same hand, put her foot in the stirrup (no, the left foot), take hold of the cantle with her right hand, and swing up. It did not work, because of the tight-fitting jodhpurs. With great effort, Miss Tisdale could get her foot in the stirrup, but then she was plain stuck.

Consuelo led the horse alongside a fair-sized boulder and had Miss Tisdale try to mount from that. It was not high enough, and, worse, it rocked and sent her tumbling. Consuelo tried to boost her, but she did not have Canuto's strength. Then she remembered a stretch of cut bank along the road a little farther on, so she led the horse to that. There she tied both horses to bushes, setting the brown alongside the bank, and gave her whole strength to helping Miss Tisdale into the saddle. As she pushed and strained, she was aware of how easy it would be to stop pushing and straining, to mount the buckskin and head for home and leave the silly woman to shift for herself. She had enough Spanish ruthlessness to have done just that under other circumstances, but now, with the oncoming storm, it was out of the question.

Consuelo lifted and strained; Miss Tisdale, flushed and embarrassed, tried to help, and only made things worse. When all pushing and straining failed, they both rested a few seconds, and then the struggle began again. The trees, the rocks, the cut bank turned pale with lightning time after time. The sky threatened to crack wide open over their heads.

An unusual situation, a course of action entered upon without reflection, will sometimes reveal to us inner thoughts and realizations that we have long kept concealed from ourselves. That happened to Consuelo at this point. As she labored under the black sky, she was keenly aware of her mountains in their splendor and their danger, but now, for the first time, she admitted to herself that they no longer sufficed, and Rociada was not secure. Something was expected of her, of all of them. Getting this absurd creature back into the saddle and to shelter was her own small part in the common, most serious, struggle to keep the ranch. It was one with what Pino had to subject himself to when he took out hunting parties for pay, and with her mother's struggle with the account books late into the night. It did not matter in the least whether Consuelo liked or loathed Miss Tisdale. She was a job, not a friend for the choosing. And this was nothing compared to the jobs her mother and brother were handling; it was up to her to do hers, and do it well, and to be ready for whatever might come along after this.

Finally Miss Tisdale was mounted, and, with the first drops of the rain pattering around them, they set off at a lope for the first farm on the road, where they took shelter under a carriage shed until the rain let up. In the Southwest, such rainstorms are usually brief. They rode home under a clearing sky, in brilliant sunshine, and with fragments of rainbow in the northwest. As they jogged along the short strip of road to the ranch, Miss Tisdale apologized for her awkwardness. Embarrassed, Consuelo answered with a commonplace. It occurred to her that this woman, however ignorant and clumsy, was a decent sort, and definitely game. Her hostility relaxed. Natural kindness and the old-established habit of hospitality began to assert themselves. When Miss Tisdale offered another apology, Consuelo told her it was not her fault; the trouble was with her unsuitable jodhpurs. They would outfit her with levis, so that she could be comfortable, and when she was ready to ride again, they would take easier, shorter trips. It might interest her to visit some of the nearer sheep camps, and she should see the Lower Ranch; the ranchhouse there was built in the authentic old Spanish style, around a square patio, with a big covered entrance you could ride through. It was almost like a castle. As she talked she planned easy rides that would keep them always within reach of workmen, sheepherders, or *vaqueros,* just in case there should be another hoisting job to be done. She and Miss Tisdale were friendly together by the time they turned in at the Bacas' gate.

Consuelo took a course in typing at school the next winter, and at the beginning of June she insisted on getting a job. She found one in a title abstractor's office in Las Vegas, where she could live with cousins. The knowledge that she was now bringing solid help to her mother, on whom she had so long and so lovingly depended, sustained her through the initial week, for she soon discovered that searching old records was not, as she had expected, interesting, and that what she had taken on was like condemning herself to a summer of pure algebra.

Love will not always be practical; it demands its own expressions. With her first pay check Consuelo made a down payment on a miniature wristwatch with a delicate silver web of a bracelet, which seemed to her to have been made especially for her mother. It was the first wristwatch that Doña Marguerite had ever had, and it would be hard to say which of them, she or Consuelo, was more delighted. For a moment, the girl could forget the chill wind that blew ever stronger. In any case, she had set her foot on the path that led in time to the office buildings of Manhattan, and hence to my own everlasting good fortune.